Community Resocialization

A New Perspective

by

James E. Garrett, M.S.W.

Associate Director, Institute
For Delinquency Control,
Instructor, St. Louis University
School of Social Service

Peter O. Rompler, M.A.

Director of
Research and Evaluation,
Institute for Delinquency Control,
St. Louis University

The Catholic University of America Press

Washington, D. C. 20017

HV
7428
.G3

Sponsored by a Training Grant from the Office of Juvenile Delinquency and Youth Development, Welfare Administration, U.S.
Department of Health, Education, and Welfare, in cooperation
with the President's Committee on Juvenile Delinquency and
Youth Crime.

Contents

Preface

T HE ACCELERATION of juvenile delinquency is a cause of alarm to the society at large. As with many other social problems the dimensions of delinquency are such as to attract national attention and a response from the federal government. At the same time, the necessity of attempting to solve the problem with something more enlightened than mere force or punishment has spurred social scientists and social workers to get at the causes of delinquency. Juvenile delinquency treatment and prevention, therefore, is rapidly being adopted as an area and responsibility of social work practice and education. This book is a significant contribution to the fulfillment of this responsibility.

Juvenile delinquency, of course, is only one form of social deviance that our society sustains. Family disorganization, economic deprivation, the cultural ghetto and the slum culture, and segregation are other examples of deviance that reflect certain underlying disorders in the society. At one time it was thought, and there are perhaps those who are still influenced by the persuasion that each form of deviance is a disparate thing unto itself with its own cause and remedy, both of which are unrelated to the cause and remedy of every other form of deviance.

A more penetrating understanding of society, however, is leading the social scientist to grasp both the horizontal and vertical interrelatedness of the many units of the social system. In its horizontal dimension, successful functioning of one social role is related to the functioning of other roles; primary and secondary groups are interdependent in their social functioning; and the successful functioning of associations and communities that span local, state and national limits depends on the functioning of other associations and communities in the total system. In its vertical dimension, the social system is a complex pattern of interrelated individuals, groups and communities, so that dysfunction at any level affects every other level.

The cause of social deviance, therefore, is not one, and is not simple, whether it is juvenile delinquency or any other deviant behavior. Any form of social deviance, therefore, is at one time and from one point of view, a cause of other patterns of deviance, at another time and from another point of view, a symptom of other deviant patterns. The gang whose hostility leads to the breaking of windows and school property is partially at least the product of neighborhood and community neglect; but the gang likewise contributes to the deterioration of neighborhood and community.

If the cause of deviant behavior is so complex, effective treatment will be complex. If the cause of a child's delinquency includes parental immaturity and family instability, street gangs, a school system unsuited to the child's needs, poverty and slums, neighborhood and community apathy, then a treatment program that disregards any one of the contributing forces is, to that extent, deficient as an instrument of treatment and prevention.

The Juvenile Delinquency Project at the Saint Louis University School of Social Service is based on this assumption: that juvenile delinquency is generally the result of a pattern of dysfunctioning at all three levels of the social system—individual, group and community; therefore effective intervention must be directed at all three levels. And the Project is based on the related assumption that the Juvenile Court, the social institution most concerned with Juvenile Corrections, is but one institution in the social system that must be mobilized if the community as a whole is to succeed in its task of the treatment and prevention of delinquency. The title of the manuscript that has issued from the Project reflects these assumptions. *Community Resocialization—A New Perspective* directs the reader's attention away from a too exclusive preoccupation with the individual delinquent to his family, neighborhood groups and the immediate community, and to the configuration of social institutions that actually or potentially are significant contributors to the life and development of every child. If these assumptions are valid, certain aspects of the

Project have implications beyond the field of Juvenile Corrections. Delinquency, family and community disorganization, ignorance, economic deprivation, the cultural ghetto and the slum culture and segregation are community problems; and they are not phenomena that are isolated one from the other. The implication is that education not only for the field of Corrections, but for every field of social work practice, requires a new perspective.

In assisting this Project the Office of Juvenile Delinquency and Youth Development has encouraged a trend in social work education and practice that is needed if society is adequately to meet the demands that confront it. By crystallizing in this present manuscript certain issues, assumptions and theories, Mr. Garrett and Mr. Rompler have made a decided contribution to Correctional practice. Not only have the authors very ably opened up certain areas of the Correctional task that must be reexamined, they have also suggested that the Juvenile Court readapt itself to a new function in a community of agencies and institutions each of which must be involved in the task of Correctional treatment and prevention.

Saint Louis University   BERNARD J. COUGHLIN, S.J.
Dean, School of Social Service

Acknowledgements

GRATEFUL ACKNOWLEDGEMENT is made to Dr. Elliot Studt for permission to use certain materials as a basis for much of the thought here developed and to the Council of Social Work Education for its interest and permission to use certain materials from its publication, "A Conceptual Approach to Teaching Materials: Illustrations From the Field of Corrections by Dr. Elliot Studt." The authors are also indebted to Assistant Professor Robert Dawson of Washington University School of Law for his critical reading of parts of the manuscript and especially to Father Bernard J. Coughlin, S.J., Dean of the School of Social Service, Saint Louis University and Project Director, for his original inspiration and encouragement in carrying through the effort.

The bulk of the work here done mostly represents the thoughts and work of many other individuals rather than the original thoughts of the authors. To all of these the authors wish to give full credit. Conceptions and thought patterns gained from Professor Gilbert Geis of Los Angeles State College in particular contributed heavily to some of the basic thinking involved. All of those who participated both as faculty and students in our workshops and institutes contributed in countless ways by sharing with us their thoughts, feelings and problems.

To merely add the credit line that the entire project was sponsored by a training grant from the Office of Juvenile Delinquency and Youth Development, Welfare Administration, U.S. Department of Health, Education and Welfare, in cooperation with the President's Committee on Juvenile Delinquency and Youth Crime, seems incomplete. It is to the understanding, interest and cooperation of individuals making up the President's Committee that we owe the existence of the Project. The President's Committee approval of the original grant proposal submitted by

Father Bernard Coughlin, S.J., its interest in permitting continuation, and its encouragement of publication of the manuscript has brought this work to fruition. Hopefully, it is in some measure a return on their investment.

JAMES E. GARRETT
PETER O. ROMPLER

Community Resocialization
A New Perspective

I. Introduction

James E. Garrett

Hopefully the massive new programs aimed at creating opportunity for youth will bring about a noticeable reduction in the increasing number of children referred to the Juvenile Court. But for those referred under existing practices to our Juvenile Correctional systems as presently operated and structured, there is not likely to be much promise of noticeable progress. Factors that prevent efficient handling of the problem are discussed in this work.

While many analyses have been made of the Juvenile Court structure, an attempt to see the juvenile delinquent in relation to a complete Correctional system was started early in 1964. This was part of an effort (begun in 1963) to devise new concepts and training materials in line with the objectives of the Probation Training Demonstration Project grant to the St. Louis University School of Social Service by the President's Committee on Juvenile Delinquency and Youth Crime.[1]

Evidence that many Correctional personnel, as well as those agencies and social institutions they dealt with, saw themselves as functioning mainly around their own agency-defined objectives as the focus of Correctional activities, became apparent early to project personnel. While this was a familiar pattern, the diverse agency representation in the Workshops and Institutes between 1963 and 1965 suggested a collection of relatively isolated units with different operational goals based on different philosophies and theories for curbing delinquency. It was almost as if each

[1] A three year, two phase project aimed at developing methods and curriculum content to improve further the training of the juvenile correctional officer. One phase gave attention to in-service training; the other to training in a school of social work and the feasibility of probation techniques widening the scope of community involvements.

were a separate auto assembly line manufacturing parts according to his own specifications and then trying to see whether they could all be pooled and assembled into a car.[2]

A closer examination of the organization and availability of resources to the various Juvenile Courts in Missouri and other sections of the country revealed a wide range of approaches to problems of juveniles. Various attitudes toward delinquency and juvenile problems were expected, but the inadequacy of resources and services in many areas raised the question of whether many of the Courts could properly be called Juvenile Courts at all. Legal nomenclature or designation does not, *per se,* make a Juvenile Court. If one considers how basic the probation or social work function is to the Juvenile Court concept, it is to be noted that many Courts show no trace of such service if one defines social work as an effective problem solving process.

Reflection on the situation pointed up the relative inadequacy in law of the Missouri Juvenile Court system. A modernized State Juvenile Code was passed by the Missouri Legislature in 1957, but as in many other states, it appears as if it was attached onto the existing judicial structure without recognition of the complexity of the task undertaken and concurrent responsibility of the Court in assuming jurisdiction under the doctrine of *parens patriae.*

A. What is the Standard?

The basic justification in law for the Court's intervention in the life of the child is that it is designated by society to act for it, to enforce value judgments on the youthful population through a legal mechanism. This "acting in the relationships of parents for the child" is further expressed in the Missouri Juvenile Code and those of other states by rather vague generalizations that:

> . . . each child coming within the jurisdiction of the court shall receive such care, guidance and control, preferably in his own home, as will conduce to the child's welfare and the best interests of the state and that when such child is removed from the control of his parents the court shall

---

[2] See William Reid, "Interagency Co-ordination in Delinquency Prevention and Control," *Social Service Review,* Vol. XXXVIII, No. 4 (December, 1964), p. 423.

secure for him care as nearly as possible equivalent to that which should have been given him by them.[3]

Thus in any case the child's welfare is deemed to be enhanced by the Court's intervention, as well as the best interests of the state, for if it is the state's welfare that is the prime consideration then the very basis of the Juvenile Code is in question. The *standard of care* is apparently whatever the Juvenile Judge says it is and that which a given community sees fit to provide. The fact that a given Juvenile Court assumes jurisdiction under these statutory directions has meant merely that some controls or admonishment of a varying nature were imposed under a judicial exercise of authority. Enhancement of the child's welfare is a matter of varying judgment when measured in terms of the quality and amount of services provided.

Many laws are written necessarily in a vague manner in order to give them the desired flexibility to meet the ever changing needs of society. It is questionable, however, if vagueness in the Juvenile Code was meant to serve as a legal refuge *for avoiding responsibility to the very child it was designed to protect.*

It it not sufficient for the Juvenile Court Judge to take it for granted that, because the statutory aim is protective and therapeutic, rather than punitive, the actual pursuit of that *aim has in fact been implemented by adequate institutions and agencies* and by dedicated and informed personnel. It must not be forgotten that the provision of protective and therapeutic programs for juvenile offenders is the *legal cornerstone* on which rests the Constitutional structure of Juvenile Court statutes.[4]

What Dean Pound recognized was that if preventive, therapeutic programs are to be implemented and rehabilitative results are to be achieved, *the Correctional system (including the Court) cannot operate in isolation.* When the objectives of the Court are fully carried out in terms of its responsibilities as defined by law, it is readily seen that its effective functioning is highly interrelated with many agencies specifically, and with the *entire community* generally.

---

[3] Missouri, *Juvenile Code* (1957), Sec. 211.011

[4] Sheldon Glueck, "Roscoe Pound and Criminal Justice," *Crime and Delinquency,* National Council on Crime and Delinquency, Vol. X, No. 4 (October, 1964), p. 340. (Emphasis added.)

Development of training methods and concepts were thus pointed toward more clearly identifying these interrelationships with other social institutions and the community with the idea of developing a view of our present Correctional facilities as a *cohesive system.*

To appropriately explore the makeup of an efficient Correctional system, various facets are considered in the following chapters. Among these are the social problems presented by the juvenile client and the resulting task of the Court. Neither the social problem nor the task of the Court can be realistically considered, however, unless they are viewed against the framework of working relationships and concepts that presently determine the limits of Juvenile Correctional practice. Therefore, the legal ramifications and the present level of agency coordination are also considered.

If we are to be concerned with the rehabilitation or resocialization of juvenile clients, then we are also concerned with how socialization takes place within our culture. This concept is dealt with in Chapter III which furnishes a complementary basis for an attempt at synthesis in terms of training in the concluding analysis. The relationship of this effort to the overall training project is developed in Chapter IV.

II. The Court and the Community

A. The Juvenile Client

As delinquency is a legally defined term rather than a sociological or clinical entity, clients in the Correctional caseload can be expected to present a wide variety of personality types and emotional adjustment.[1] The fact that it is legally defined does not guarantee anything except that it is the result of attempts by various State Legislatures to define standards of youthful behavior within a certain specified age range and to establish categories for their classification.

Delinquency definitions are far from uniform. In some states there is no specification; in others, a long list. Both upper and lower age limits vary and in some states the upper age limits for girls are higher than for boys. As with most adult criminal codes, just who is designated a criminal or a delinquent is a matter of legislative caprice, judicial discretion and police efficiency. Unlike adult criminal codes, however, unless the child commits an act which would be a crime if he were an adult, his delinquency is generally a matter of uncodified value judgment. To regard those who are found delinquent as a different order of being from the alleged law abiding child is no more valid than the idea that the average lay person in the community is particularly knowledgeable concerning human behavior in general.

Thus, many factors operate to determine the kinds of children referred to the Court for hearing and adjudication, ranging from geography, to the training, education and personal biases of the police, Court intake officials, and the ability of the Court and police to withstand pressures from powerful community groups and influential persons to get the Correctional task defined in a way which supports their interests.

[1] Council on Social Work Education, *Casebook in Correctional Work* (New York: Council on Social Work Education, 1958), p. 9.

7

The various definitions may or may not even mention delinquency as such, but in most instances a broad grant of power is given to the Juvenile Court to declare virtually any form of youthful behavior which the public regards as deviant, as delinquent. It is also legally defined in the sense that a Judge or judicial officer makes decisions as to what it is in terms of the standards he wishes to set or reflect as the case may be. The Missouri Juvenile Code is an example of language used as a basis of a codified definition of a delinquent. Sec. 211.031 provides:

Except as otherwise provided herein, the Juvenile Court shall have exclusive original jurisdiction in proceedings:
1. Involving any child who may be within the county who is alleged to be in need of care and treatment because:
   a. The parents or other persons legally responsible for the care and support of the child neglect or refuse to provide proper support, education which is required by law, medical, surgical or other care necessary for his well-being; except that reliance by a parent, guardian or custodian upon remedial treatment other than medical or surgical treatment for a child shall not be construed as neglect when the treatment is recognized or permitted under the laws of this state; or
   b. The child is otherwise without proper care, custody or support; or
   c. The behavior, environment or associations of the child are injurious to his welfare or to the welfare of others; or
   d. The child is alleged to have violated a state law or municipal ordinance.

After a consideration of the social problems involved and some of the aspects of making a legal category to deal with the varying problems of adolescents, we are naturally led to a consideration of the task of the Juvenile Court which is discussed in the next section.

B. Task of the Court

The function of the Juvenile Court is to determine when society has the right to enter into a child's life, and when such is the case to deal with him on an individualized basis.[2]

[2] See Merritt Gilman and Alice M. Low, *Training for Juvenile Probation Officers* (Children's Bureau Publication No. 398-1962), p. 22.

As noted in the previous section, the Juvenile Court is expected by the community to assume the function of the care and protection of children in the face of a situation where other community institutions have either failed or refused to assume the traditional responsibilities of child care.[3] (It is to be noted that various Juvenile Courts take somewhat different views of this function.) The question is not so much whether the Court actually carries out the service itself or delegates it to others, but rather the fact that it enters into the gigantic task of becoming the disciplinarian, the child rearer and the social arbiter of hundreds of children. The Juvenile Judge is responsible to the community for the basic decisions as to the policies of his Court, the types of control over children assumed, and the regulation of personnel employed by the Court. However, he can only operate within the types, amount and quality of the resources allotted to him by the community or state and his own knowledge or comprehension of the task.

The growth in latitude of children's Courts is a recognition of the fact that certain families have abdicated their responsibilities over children. It must also be recognized that *the so called failing family is frequently victimized by conditions and circumstances beyond its control.*[4]

Thus, while society expects something to be done to or for the delinquent by the Court to change his behavior, or at least cease his unacceptable behavior, it does not spell out specifically just how the Court is to do this in terms of procedures or duties. Society sets up certain explicit or implicit goals that the (Juvenile Court in this instance) is expected to pursue. *It has not usually seen itself as part of the problem, either as producing it or making possible a solution.* Rather, society has demanded *social control* by assigning responsibility to the police, parents, and various Correctional agencies, but never appears to recognize that *the achievement of the very control it demands requires constant participation on its part* in all of its many aspects.

---

[3] Gilbert Geis and Herbert A. Bloch, *Man, Crime, and Society* (New York: Random House, 1962), p. 412.

[4] *Ibid.* (Emphasis added.)

An offender comes to the correctional agency because of an act resulting from distorted relations between himself and others in his society. All the participants in the malfunctioning social situation leading to his offense have contributed to the destructive outcome: the offender himself, his significant others, the social institutions to which he has been exposed, and the community that permits conditions that encourage offending behavior.[5]

If we accept that deviant behavior or crimes are invariably reflective of and responsive to a given social order and cultural organization at a given period in their historic development and that deviant behavior of a certain type is only possible in terms of a given sociocultural matrix, then we accept that certain forms of deviant behavior occur only because society allows certain conditions to exist or not to exist.

Society assigns the responsibility of control and rehabilitation of individual offenders to Correctional agencies. Dr. Elliot Studt defines this service as "resocialization," stating that such a process must use controls over an individual's behavior and over the social experiences to which he is exposed while he establishes new patterns for social functioning, just as controls are exercised over a small child by the family and schools that provide his early socializing experiences.[6]

Thus Dr. Studt suggests a graded process of controls over the significant variables that determine an individual's social behavior. This *ability to use controls while providing training in new and more acceptable behavior patterns* is then one of the jobs in the Juvenile Court. Control is necessary for a variety of reasons. The community demands and needs protection from potentially dangerous behavior of identified offenders. But the *resocializing process* is not likely to occur unless control over the individual and the factors allowing the process to take place is exercised in a manner meeting the needs of the individual delinquent. Therefore, another major task of the Juvenile Court responsibility *is to gauge and diagnose accurately the individual problem in social functioning and devise a plan of appropriate treatment.* It is therefore to be noted that the probation officer

---

[5] Elliot Studt, "Correctional Services (Social Work Practice In)," *Encyclopedia of Social Work*, Vol. XV (National Association of Social Workers, 1965), p. 220.
[6] *Ibid.*

himself will usually act as the coordinator of treatment rather than the exclusive treator.

It is evident that the moral behavior desired of treated offenders cannot occur in a social vacuum since moral behavior requires a supporting community as well as a person who seeks to contribute to the community. The Correctional task is not completed until the offender is restored to viable interaction in his *personal*[7] community. The task of restoration requires the active participation of the offender's community.[8]

Dr. Studt states that *resocialization* thus is a two-way proposition. Furthermore it does not take place by being imposed upon an offender, nor can it be based on fear. The penalties and sanctions imposed by society for failing to conform have little meaning if one has a different set of values. Resocialization depends upon the experience of being accepted, loved and cared for. This leads to the capacity and, therefore, the ability to sacrifice one's personal desires for others. Thus, the task of the Juvenile Court is one of integrating a legally and morally degraded nonconformer into a supporting social matrix which is designed to allow change, *because in relation* to the offender, *society* is changed.

From the offender's point of view he will have been socially redefined as a person whose restoration to community membership is important and who warrants the investment of community resources.[9]

Dr. Studt is implying in no uncertain terms that all of the characteristics of the correction action and the community affect the client directly as well as determine the success of supervision. Thus, the Correctional worker is building on strengths, not only from the youngster, but from his personal community and relationships with people. The worker and the Juvenile Court must be in the mainstream of community life, constantly evaluating the total community and its resources to know whether or not it

[7] Personal community in the field services is defined by Dr. Studt as the significant persons among the offender's family, his peers, his employment associates and the community agencies to which he is related. *Ibid.,* pp. 221-222.

[8] Elliot Studt, *A Conceptual Approach to Teaching Materials* (New York: Council on Social Work Education, March, 1965), p. 11. (Emphasis added.)

[9] Studt, *loc. cit.,* "Correctional Services (Social Work Practice In)."

can provide opportunities for a normal life for clients, and to allow for effective support in time of crisis.

The Court is related to the community in the following ways:

a. The community sets certain standards with which probation officers and the Court identify.

b. The Court must have realistic and extensive knowledge of the power structure and of economics and political organization of community life in order to know what can be accomplished. (This is both in relation to its overall program and the individual client.)

c. The Court must have knowledge of roles of other agencies in the community in order to integrate properly its functions with theirs. Overlapping functions are shared with other agencies in the community in making decisions about Correctional clients.

d. Each juvenile client is seen as the center of a whole complex web of interactions in the community—all of which contribute to the fact that he behaves as a delinquent. The delinquent interacts with these persons in a framework determined not only by his tendencies to be delinquent, but also by the culture of his neighborhood, the kinds of opportunities which are available and the impersonal policies of the official agencies to which he is related. The Juvenile Court, and more specifically the probation officer, can be seen as the individualizing link between the delinquent and his community.[10]

e. It should be the function of the Court to provide community leadership aimed at encouraging and helping the community develop resources.

f. The Juvenile Court is a focus for public attention and for the efforts of influential persons and groups to get the Correctional task defined in a way which supports their interests. Different persons and groups have different and sometimes conflicting values and interests. Courts and Correctional administrators are under continual pressure to act in compromise or contradictory fashion. The Court must

[10] See Gilman and Low, *op. cit.*, p. 69.

be prepared to justify each decision legally and to public opinion.[11]

g. In that the Court assumes protection and works for the enhancement of the child's welfare and in effect becomes a community parent, it is directly related to community problems and those persons and conditions having to do with them.

h. The Juvenile Court and Correctional workers must co-ordinate decision-making so that treatment needs of individual clients are recognized without neglecting the protection of the community.

i. If the emphasis of the treatment plan of the Court is shifted from attempting to convert the lower class delinquent to middle class values to providing more opportunity for the delinquent, then the need for a broad relationship with the community is clear.

j. Effectiveness of the Juvenile Court and its services is greatly affected by its own morale. This depends on several factors, a major one of which is the level of performance with which it is permitted to discharge its responsibility to clientele and the community.

C. Legal Ramifications and Connotations

1. Power of the Juvenile Court

Courts have a unique characteristic as social institutions in our society. Society entrusts to them the ultimate sanction of compulsion, the power to make decisions which organized society will back up with force if necessary.

This force of the Courts to make binding decisions is a tremendous one. Here is power, enforceable coercion, over people's lives, the power to order lives, to make devastating mistakes sometimes, without their having the freedom to accept or reject the proposed solution to a problem. . . .

Power is always in its very nature dangerous. Some controls on the arbitrary use of power exist when power is inherent in knowledge, when

[11] See *Casebook in Correctional Work, op. cit.,* pp. 6-7.

power is exercised within a philosophy of respect for the individual human person, or a legal system which insures a fair hearing.[12]

We have earlier referred to the wide discretion granted to the Juvenile Courts and the comments made by Younghusband are particularly in point.[13]

Younghusband further notes that we cannot comfort ourselves by thinking about our *good intentions* when we consider this power aspect of the Juvenile Courts because they alone do not guarantee the constructive and fair use of power. She states:

> This power situation is not fundamentally different whether young people are brought before a Court for protection or whether they are charged with criminal offenses. There are other reasons which may make this latter practice undesirable, but whatever name we give to things— and we have a touching belief that we can alter the nature of something by changing its name—the fact of this ultimate sanction of coercion remains. The power to send children away from their homes, to break up families, to impose various conditions if the delinquent or wayward or neglected youngster stays at home—these things remain inherent in any Juvenile Court system, no matter how or for what stated reasons the state brings children before Courts.
>
> The real heart of this dilemma is that there is no escape from this exercise of power, the power vested in Courts to make binding decisions between one person and another or between society and the individual. It is generally agreed to be necessary to take forcible steps to protect some children from some parents. It is also agreed to be necessary to restrain young people who break the rules of society. But, given the recognition of this need to coerce, the parallel necessity for safeguards immediately becomes apparent.[14]

While the Courts have held the Juvenile Codes of various states Constitutional, they have not held that the Constitutional rights of due process of law and equal protection of the laws do not apply to children. The issue is whether the Constitutional rights of criminal defendants should not also be applied to juveniles? It may be, as some people predict, that the U.S. Supreme

[12] Eileen L. Younghusband, "The Dilemma of the Juvenile Court," p. 12. Reproduced with permission by the U.S. Dept. of Health, Education, and Welfare, *Social Service Review* (Chicago: The University of Chicago Press, March, 1959).

[13] Much could be said relating to the power inherent in the knowledge of juvenile courts and the fairness of the legal procedures used in them, but only those aspects directly relating to the community will be touched upon here.

[14] Younghusband, *loc. cit.*

Court will require that certain of all Constitutional rights be recognized in Juvenile Court. But unless and until that time comes, the Juvenile Courts are free to apply none, all, or some of the rights in the sense that neither adequate precedent nor adequate judicial review are presently available.[15]

The question is raised then, as to what are the checks and balances on the Juvenile Court if all the above is true?

Unlike the Constitutional guarantees in the Bill of Rights and in many State Constitutions, such as the right to counsel and the privilege against self-incrimination, the right of appeal is not a right at all in the Constitutional sense. The Supreme Court of the U.S. has held that denial of appeal in a state criminal case does not offend the Constitution and there are innumerable state court decisions holding that the right to review (of juvenile court proceedings) is not essential to due process of law, but is a matter of grace.[16]

Thus appellate review of state Court decisions is not a federal Constitutional necessity and some jurisdictions do not provide it. While the overwhelming majority of states do provide appellate review, the use made of it and the traditions and practices surrounding it appear to make it a vehicle of questionable effectiveness. The general attitude of Appellate Courts, the lack of adequate records, the legislative delegation of broad discretion to the Juvenile Judge, and provisions for competent stenographic transcripts prevent broad review.[17]

While much more could be said, the intention here is only to state the general problem. The following summarizes the legal situation of the child in the Juvenile Court.

1. Constitutional provisions and safeguards are allegedly withdrawn from the child, because the Court is supposed to be looking out for his interests.

---

[15] See Kent *vs*. United States, 86 Sup. Ct. 1045 (1966).

[16] Addison M. Bowman, "Appeals from Juvenile Courts," *Crime and Delinquency*, National Council on Crime and Delinquency, Vol. XI, No. 1 (January, 1965), p. 63.

[17] While appellate review is not a Constitutional necessity, the United States Supreme Court has recently held that if a state provides appellate review it must appoint counsel for indigent criminal appellants and secure a transcript of the Trial Court proceedings for them free of charge. If no transcript is made of the Trial Court proceedings, as in some Juvenile Courts, then neither the indigent nor the wealthy has it as the basis for appeal. See Douglas vs. California, 372U.S.353 (1963). Griffin vs. Illinois, 351U.S.12 (1959). Lane vs. Brown 372U.S.477 (1963). Draper vs. Washington 372U.S.487 (1963).

2. The child is especially vulnerable and in need of protection and representation of his interests.

3. A greater amount of administrative discretion is used here than in any other Court. Very little judicial review or other checks and balances are exercised to control use of this discretion.

4. The Juvenile Court is a relatively new mechanism in the law and there are comparatively few precedents set up to guide it.

Over the centuries we have evolved a highly sophisticated legal system, while our diagnostic and treatment systems are at a quite different, even rudimentary and fragmentary stage of development. Moreover, those who serve in Juvenile Courts have varying degrees of competence to do so, coupled with widely differing views about the function of Courts as social institutions and, therefore, of their responsibilities and aims in relation to the individual offenders. This means that there tends to be no such thing as a Juvenile Court system in a given county, but rather a broad legal framework within which each specific court develops its own individuality, its social climate, its ethos. The result is that we are abandoning the certain ties of a rigid legal system without yet being able to substitute another kind of certainty based upon scientifically determined diagnosis and treatment.[18]

5. Children are more impressionable and more highly susceptible to molding. If their first contact with the law as represented by the Juvenile Court does not appear to protect their interests, this very impression may be the basis of their conception of the law and Courts throughout their life.[19]

Dean Roscoe Pound in commenting on this point remarked that:

. . . The powers of the Star Chamber were a trifle in comparison with those of our Juvenile Courts and Courts of Domestic Relations. It is well known that too often the placing of a child in a home or even in an

[18] Younghusband, op. cit., p. 11.

[19] It might be contended that due process of law requires that court procedures give the child an appearance of fairness as well as being fair in reality. In this connection a recent pilot project indicates that juvenile offenders have extremely accurate perception and memories of the events occurring at the juvenile court hearing, contrary to the theory that they are too frightened to remember anything. See Lipsitt, Judge-Boy Communications in the Juvenile Court (National Council of Juvenile Court Judges, 1963).

institution is done casually, perfunctorily or even arbitrarily. Moreover, effective preventive work through these Courts requires looking into much more than the bad external conditions of a household, such as poverty or neglect or lack of discipline. Internal conditions, a complex of habits, attitudes and reactions, may have to be dealt with and this means *administrative treatment* of the most intimate affairs of life. Even with the most superior personnel, these tribunals call for legal checks.[20]

Pound's point of administrative treatment means heavy reliance by the Juvenile Judge on administrative personnel to help him in administering the various functions of the Court. This can mean personnel in his own Court or in other agencies to which segments of authority are delegated. The wide discretionary powers of the Court are thus translatable into *wide administrative discretion* dependent upon the policies of the individual Judge. While the Judge remains directly responsible to the community for the policies of the Court, this does not make the actions and policies of the probation officer any less responsible.

The case is thus made that if a hard look ought to be taken and stringent standards ought to be imposed on any branch or mechanism of the law, it ought to be the Juvenile Court. Yet for reasons to be discussed, it is not.

2. Existing Legal Practice and Structure

As with most humans, things that lawyers do not understand may be threatening to them. No less appears to be true of the legal profession as concerns the Juvenile Court. This explanation as to why the legal profession has not met its obligations by admitting the existence of the Juvenile Court and developing an understanding of its theory of operation and practice appears to have some validity.

Not many in the legal profession seem able or willing to give an adequate explanation of the doctrine of *parens patriae* and define its limits and ramifications. Learned papers appear occasionally, but the question whether the Court is civil, partly punish-

---

[20] Sheldon Glueck, "Roscoe Pound and Criminal Justice," *Crime and Delinquency*, National Council on Crime and Delinquency, Vol. X, No. 4 (October, 1964), p. 314. (Emphasis added.)

ing, or whether civil or criminal rules of procedure apply, does not appear to be generally settled at all.

It may be that:

the fact that Juvenile Court work is a minor responsibility in most jurisdictions, may be interpreted as indicating that the job can be done on this basis. Perhaps a more realistic assessment, however, would be that although the philosophy of the Juvenile Court has achieved universal acceptance, it has been integrated into the existing judicial Court structure without recognition of the complexity of the job assignment.[21]

It is regrettable that most Juvenile Court problems are not susceptible of solution by the pronouncements of an aloof, independent judiciary or the dispensing of justice according to the calculated specifics of the adult criminal code, based on a body of precedents and traditions that give security, stability, and guidance to the Judge. The Juvenile Judge is involved with theories of child behavior and rearing when he assumes jurisdiction. When he makes a finding of delinquency, dependency or neglect, he and his Court become responsible to do something about it. Unless the Court is successful in passing the child along to a state institution, *the Court remains involved in the child's life*. The point might be made that legislative grants of broad discretion to Juvenile Courts is premised on the assumption that adequate treatment resources are available and that broad discretion is needed to put these resources to effective use. The assumption that adequate resources exist is clearly false. Therefore, the inadequacy of Juvenile Court resources is not only tragic *per se*, but also places the Juvenile Court on unsound legal foundations.

Judges taking on the Juvenile Court job may react in different ways to the ambiguities, the frustrations and the new responsibilities. Some may react by feeling that they have become captive of the social worker. "For the vast majority of these judges, serving only part time in juvenile and family matters, the title of 'juvenile court judge' is more descriptive of a state of mind than

---

[21] Shirley D. McCune and Daniel L. Skoler, "Juvenile Court Judges in the United States, Part I: A National Profile," *Crime and Delinquency,* National Council on Crime and Delinquency, Vol. XI, No. 2 (April, 1965), p. 126.

of a discrete group in the judicial hierarchy."[22] Although the authors of this statement are referring to the structure of the legal system which provides for several duties of a given Judge, one of which may be serving as Juvenile Judge, it is evident that for various reasons the idea exists in many jurisdictions independent of the ability, comprehension and will to successfully execute the office.

3. Purpose of the Court

The Juvenile Court in assuming the protection and care of children makes a judicial determination of what their needs are. It not only attempts to gauge what those needs are, but it determines what will be done about them. Thus it has the authority similar to Criminal Courts to order a change in the lives of the individuals before it. The difficulty lies in the translation of that authority into achieving the actual change. *There is no specific cut-off point involving problem solving or control in performing the task assumed by the Juvenile Court.* Problems of any given disadvantaged person are all of a piece, connected and derivative of one another.

If the Court understands and appreciates the various factors which led to the poor adjustment of the delinquent within the community, then it has the responsibility of dealing with those pressures as they impinge on the behavior of the youngster. In intervening, treating, protecting and caring for the child, it may be necessary to deal with *community influences* which have made or helped to make him what he is.

The family may have to be the unit of work, even if the legal unit in the legal proceeding is the child. Thus juvenile probation and parole are not child-centered to the exclusion of parents. This raises the question whether the probation agencies of the Juvenile Court are equipped to do family case work?

There are several problems encountered here.

a. The Court attempts to work in an area where it usually has jurisdiction over only one individual.

---

[22] *Ibid.,* p. 122.

   b. Many skills, resources and specialized knowledge are in-
      volved in family problem situations.
   c. The community influences upon a child may be many. They
      exist because the community exists and are no more separa-
      ble or less complicated than the society that forms the
      community. *For the Court to deal with them means to
      deal with the community.*
   d. There are legal deadlines to be met and Correctional case-
      loads are of a size that has not permitted time for this
      type of treatment. To ask the Correctional worker to func-
      tion in this manner is asking him to perform an impossible
      task.

If we recognize that the mechanism we have created in the
Juvenile Court is one that is quite different from the more rigid
body of traditional law and familiar traditional mechanisms, we
also understand that considerable thought and planning must go
into making it the competent, keen-edged, flexible tool it must
be to serve its purpose. The problem here is the forging of formal
law and formal law structure into a tool of informal social control.

If the Juvenile Court is to uphold the responsibility imposed
on it by law and to intervene in the child's life in the best interests
of the child and the state, it seems reasonable to require that it
adequately equip itself for the task. If the Juvenile Court is to
be allowed the privilege of intervention and unparalleled administrative discretion, the fact that administrative decision bears
a judicial stamp does not change the requirement to meet the
test of quality and provision for the necessary resources to do
its job.

From the foregoing statements it is logical to state that the
Juvenile Court is indeed a unique Court. It is given a unique
grant of powers, unique discretion, and it uniquely relies heavily
upon administrative decision, and, hopefully, on unique competence. While it is not desirable that the Court should become
a kind of family service agency or child welfare agency, but
rather it should be used as a last resort service.

That is, the Court should come into the picture only when questions of restraint and compulsion necessarily arise. To use it otherwise is to confuse its proper function in society. The essential purpose of the Court is to enforce social controls, to set limits to conduct which society regards as undesirable. This is different from the purpose of clinics or family agencies.[23]

The point here is that the Juvenile Court remains a Court, however unique, with essentially traditional Court functions. It is a legal entity in the life of a child for purposes of protection and social control for adjustment between the offender and society. It may be the primary means of remedying this breakdown of relations.

4. Relative Competence of the Court to Make Decisions

To fulfill all these previously mentioned requirements requires skill, and the question is raised where do we get it? Various sections of this paper have dealt with the many aspects as to why the Juvenile Court job is different. Because the job is different it follows that it requires a new breed of judicial officer.

The fact that law schools in the United States have failed to provide training for this task is significant, but in no way lessens the need or deals with the problems. Certainly, if law schools were to emphasize more Juvenile Court law and practice in legal education, or at least make it available, this would not only prepare attorneys to serve in the Courts, but encourage them to accept Juvenile Court responsibilities with less resistance. Perhaps it might even provide more ability to assist their clients and the aims of the legal profession in general. The question of education is considered by McCune and Skoler in the following.

Is legal education alone sufficient for adequate functioning in the role of a Juvenile Court judge? Many judges participating in the study[24] indicated that one of their most pressing problems in Juvenile Court work was lack of knowledge about proper methods of handling cases. This would suggest the need for more specialized education programs for aspiring Juvenile Court judges or the establishment of in-service training for aspiring

[23] Younghusband, *op. cit.*, p. 14.

[24] "Juvenile Court Judges in the United States: A National Profile." This article and the study on which it is based derive from research conducted for a demonstration training project of the National Council of Juvenile Court Judges supported by a grant of the National Institute of Mental Health, U.S. Department of Health, Education, and Welfare (Grant MH-00998).

Juvenile Court judges when they assume office. The importance of behavioral science to the work of the Court is unquestioned. It would be reasonable to expect that the judge, vested with ultimate decision authority in "treatment" determination, should not have at least enough familiarity with this field to be able to assess and understand the diagnostic and treatment recommendations of his behavioral science experts (psychologists, psychiatrists, probation officers).[25]

The peculiar traits, disposition, biases and habits of the particular Judge will, then, often determine what he decided to be the law. In this respect Judges do not differ from other men. F. S. Schiller enumerates the following factors as likely to influence judicial decisions. "The judges' education, general and legal; their family and personal associations, wealth and social position; their legal and political affiliations and opinions, their intellectual and temperamental traits."[26]

Not only is it reasonable to assume that the Juvenile Judge should have enough familiarity with this field to be able to assess and understand the diagnostic and treatment recommendation, but that the Judge is comfortable enough when surrounded by persons of different training and disciplines that he is not unduly threatened or intimidated by unfamiliar terminology and philosophies. Also, decisions concerning the range of administrative discretion in a given case can properly be made only if relative competence of treatment facilities and personnel are known. The Judge is thus involved in more than the usual weighing of evidence concerning relative mental health or other familiar courtroom procedures known to traditional law. He is here vested with ultimate decision authority with respect to treatment and its various efficacies.

Various "treatment" decisions of administrative or social work personnel may impinge upon the individual rights of the child. The Judge is charged with protecting these rights. He can best protect rights when he is thoroughly familiar with the potential of various administrative recommendations.

To discharge this function as Juvenile Courts are now constituted, the

---

[25] McCune and Skoler, *op. cit.,* p. 129.

[26] Jerome Frank, *Law and the Modern Mind* (Garden City, New York: Doubleday & Company, Inc., 1963), pp. 119, 120, 123.

Judge, in addition to applying legal expertise, may be called upon to perform the duties of an administrator, a rehabilitation expert, a community organizer and even a politician. Some of these functions may be "unofficial" and, in fortunately situated Courts, there may be a variety of professional resources to provide investigation assistance, diagnostic analyses, treatment recommendations and administrative assistance. The Judge remains caretaker of the system and retains ultimate decision authority, on both the adjudication and the treatment level.[27]

The social worker bears no less responsibility to demonstrate competence. The fact that social workers state that they base their judgments on *expert social evaluation* of what is best for any given client does not avoid the continuing necessity to question this competence against a framework of individual rights.

The use of unshared and largely intuitive procedures by different workers appears to be predominant in the Correctional field. These tactics are frequently vague and ambiguous to the worker and they are not based on the available empirical evidence regarding the nature of offenders. Instead they are compounded out of gross behavioral theories and speculative hunches arrived at by trial and error in the work setting.[28]

If the Juvenile Court job does encompass all these aspects and does not fulfill its function without making adequate provision for them, then the judicial structure has served as trappings to give respectability and sanction to an idea in name only. While serving its present questionable function, the Court unconsciously appears to have combined with the community in an illicit pact to defraud the juvenile and deprive him and his family of their rights under the sonorous pronouncement of "in the child's best interests."

5. Collective Responsibility

Thus far this section has considered various legal aspects of the Juvenile Court. One consideration was power, the broad grant of power given by the community to the Court. Also taken up was the fact that the law had not provided appropriate checks

---

[27] McCune and Skoler, *op. cit.,* p. 122.

[28] Donald C. Gibbons, "Some Notes on Treatment Theory in Corrections," *The Social Service Review* (Chicago: The University of Chicago Press, September, 1962), Vol. XXXVI, No. 3, p. 296.

and balances. The law and law schools were taken to task for not becoming more interested or getting their own house in order and social workers were questioned as to evidence validating their use of alleged professional treatment theories. The community was connected to the Juvenile Court, but its specific obligations were not defined.

Like most institutions in a democracy, along with the granting of power to the Court by the community, there is a concurrent responsibility to see that it is properly used. Crime and delinquency are viewed as offenses against society. Hence the community has a definite responsibility to support law abiding conduct. This is to provide the necessary preventive and rehabilitative agencies and to demand a high order of performance from those in charge.

It is not the law schools or the legal profession alone which are said to bear the major responsibility for the present plight of the Juvenile Court. To the extent that lawyers and teachers of law are part of the community they must bear their share. However, it is the *collective community* itself which is necessary to the process of change.

When social relationships are transforming daily, legal relationships cannot be expressed in enduring form. Many factors are operative in the transition from an agrarian society to an industrialized-urbanized society. Disorganization at many levels of societal structure is an inevitable effect of basic change in the socio-economic system. New patterns must be devised. The Juvenile Court idea was evolved to illustrate that we have humane intentions toward children when delinquency came to be recognized as a social rather than an individual problem. This "socialization" of legal procedures did not take place independently of community thought, but rather as a result of it.

Law is a product of human society subject to change and growth just as any other part of an organic whole. Laws governing the Juvenile Court and juvenile delinquency are not the unique responsibility of agencies, institutions or parents. All the factors which contribute to both came out of the collective community. The community has a particular and direct responsibility for the children and youth and their families with special problems which affect their ability to provide for themselves and to be contributing and productive citizens in our society. Considering the complexity of modern society, communities do not become interested or involved with special problems, unless the problem becomes highly destructive or especially widely understood. Usually change takes place as the result of crises, unless a calculated organized effort is made to effect it. A discussion of agency coordination and change is further developed in the next section.

D. Problems of Interagency Cooperation

If we accept that juvenile delinquency is multidetermined and that in any individual case a variety of treatment techniques and resources may be necessary, we can point up the very practical necessity for interagency cooperation and coordination. In fact, the very conception of law, of a government of laws and not of men, calls for a *system*. A system which is the result of many minds and tested experience. When the Juvenile Court becomes a legal entity in the life of a child and assumes responsibilities under the doctrine of *parens patriae*, it is then logical to assume that it does so as part of a system, a system that gains its authority and jurisdiction from its ability to provide better for the child's welfare, while fully protecting all his present and future rights. It has been assumed that whatever is necessary in the way of organization of services and resources is readily available to accomplish the objectives defined as the legal basis for jurisdiction and intervention.

However, if we look at the level of coordination of existing resources which could contribute to the treatment, control and prevention of delinquency, we see that it is so poor that an integrated attack on the problem is not possible.[29] Because of this in very few communities has the idea of the Juvenile Court even been tried or has the Juvenile Court been permitted to assume its

---

[29] National Institute of Mental Health and Children's Bureau, U. S. Dept. of Health, Education and Welfare, *Report to the Congress on Juvenile Delinquency* (Washington, D.C.: U.S. Government Printing Office, 1957), p. 9.

affirmative obligations. The fact that the Court has not done so, lays the foundation for discussion in this section.

Agencies of their own accord can and do develop referral agreements and sponsor joint programs. A theory of how and why such interaction occurs is perhaps a preliminary step toward understanding the role of the coordinating agency. . . .[30]

Cooperative arrangements among agencies may be viewed as a system of exchanges. In order to achieve their objectives, organizations must possess or control certain resources—personnel, services, funds and etc. Since most agencies do not possess all the resources needed to achieve their goals, they frequently turn to one another to obtain them.[31]

Communities and states vary widely in their distribution of resources to Juvenile Courts. But the Juvenile Court in and of itself does not usually possess the resources necessary to do its job, in any given community. However, our point is a broader one and revolves around the fact that in order to do the job of re-socialization of the individual, the Juvenile Court needs the *community as a collective resource.*

The importance of agency and institutional goals then becomes highly pertinent to our discussion. Wm. Reid defines organizational activity, including coordination, "as directed toward achieving goals of concern to the organization,"[32] however the organization defines them.

Viewing coordination as an exchange through which agencies attempt to achieve their goals, forces consideration of what their goals actually are. In this type of analysis one need not assume that the most important agency goals be in furthering the welfare of the community or that agencies in a community are bound together in a closely knit system in which each seeks similar goals through different means. Much of the prescriptive writing on coordination assumes that agencies have or should have common goals. It is another matter, however, to examine agency goals for what they are, without prior assumptions or illusions.[33]

[30] William Reid, "Interagency Co-ordination in Delinquency Prevention and Control," *The Social Service Review* (Chicago: The University of Chicago Press, 1964), Vol. XXXVIII, p. 418.

[31] *Ibid.,* p. 419, quoting Sol Levin and Paul E. White, "Exchange as a Conceptual Framework for the Study of Interorganizational Relationships," *Administrative Science Quarterly,* V (March, 1961), pp. 583-601.

[32] Reid, "Interagency Co-ordination in Delinquency Prevention and Control," *op. cit.,* p. 419.

[33] *Ibid.*

Probably no other field lacks the organizational integration around a common set of values as does Correction. Many factors peculiar to our legal system and governmental structure do not readily lend themselves to cooperation or coordination. Dean Roscoe Pound writes:

. . . The agencies of justice are more or less independent of one another, and there are some which continually hinder or thwart each other, or . . . lend each other little or no aid. Each state, each county, each municipality, each Court, each prosecutor, each police organization is likely to go its independent course, with little or no regard for what the other is doing . . . state and federal agencies have concurrent powers, they seldom concur in any effective cooperation. When there is but one jurisdiction involved, police, public prosecutors, and the coroner may proceed with parallel investigation, or investigations that cross each other or may even hinder each other, as the exigencies of politics, quest for publicity, or zeal for the public service may dictate.[34]

Sheldon Glueck notes that the Court system itself further concerned Dean Pound.

It has been pointed out more than once of late, that a Juvenile Court passing on delinquent children; a court of divorce jurisdiction entertaining a suit for divorce, alimony and custody of children; a court of common-law jurisdiction entertaining an action for necessaries furnished to an abandoned wife by a grocer; and a criminal court or domestic relations court in prosecution for desertion of a wife and child—that all of these courts might be dealing piecemeal at the same time with the difficulties of the same family.[35]

The various correctional agencies are expected somehow to restore a given offender as a conforming and contributing member of a community. The process used accomplishing this is described by Dr. Elliot Studt.

These subtasks are defined usually as discrete, unrelated activities, mutually exclusive. This kind of heterogeneity of task assignment and organizational goals has many consequences for the structure of correctional organizations and the practice of social work within them.[36]

Thus the following factors appear to define the present status

[34] Glueck, op. cit., p. 325. Quoting Dean Roscoe Pound.
[35] Ibid., quoted in Pound, "The Place of the Family Court in the Judicial System," 5 NPPA J. 162, 167-68 (1959).
[36] Studt, A Conceptual Approach to Teaching Materials, op. cit., p. 11.

of the field of Correction and consequently to a great extent that of Juvenile Correction.

1. The Lack of Organizational Integration Around a Common Set of Values.

One of the largest factors appears to be the *varying philosophies of Correction*. Revenge, the satisfaction of a desire for vengeance and the common belief that fear of the pain of stigma, imprisonment or death is vitally necessary to the control of behavior, constitute an inheritance of tradition that has governed most correctional thought for centuries. "Only gradually during the last one hundred years has *service* been introduced as a means to manage the social problems of moral deviance; and that service is still provided primarily for those individuals who have made their moral difficulty clear by offending against the criminal law."[37]

2. "Fair Game" for Vested Interests.

A resulting mixture of goals and objectives, the relative independence of most agencies of justice in the framework of state and local laws, leaves considerable administrative discretion in the treatment of convicted and adjudicated individuals. Other factors such as the different job objectives of policing organizations, the need for security, and various stringent legal requirements all contribute to the opportunity for the exercise of countless personal viewpoints and aims. The opportunity for personal or political gain as well as public attention and loss of present status or power produce a continually shifting array of Correctional organizations. For this reason, Corrections is a prime target for vested interests.

3. The Nature of Corrections Itself.

Moral deviance from the norm appears to provide vicarious satisfactions and interest for some, as well as relief from boredom from everyday routine for others. Hostile, acting-out, aggressive

[37] *Ibid.*

individuals provide a focus for material by the news media as well as fulfill the need of the public for scapegoats. In addition, correctional decisions are often of an emergency nature because of the circumstances surrounding the client and the nature of his deviance. Decisions often involve the taking of a calculated risk on the part of the agency or officer involved. When the community feels it is over-endangered by an individual offender, considerable reaction is likely to follow.

4. Variance of Needs.

Because of the varying needs and their resultant interaction with countless community and personal situations contributing to each individual's peculiar brand of deviance, a variety of skills and resources are required to deal with it. To serve these situations a repertoire of intervention activities is necessary and many persons become associated in making decisions about any one given individual.

5. Lack of Correctional Job Descriptions and Treatment Typology.

Because the Correctional field has not been able to unite, and lacks cohesiveness and purpose, it has been unable to agree upon certain typologies of treatment procedures. Failing to do this, it is understandable why the necessary training and skills for jobs in the Correctional field of practice have not been formulated.

6. Lack of Judicial Review.

Until recently, there has been relatively little review of the treatment of convicted or adjudicated individuals. Except in cases where certain types of transgression of individual rights have occurred and were able to make their way to the Courts, there has been little judicial review of administrative supervision. Types of treatment employed appear as varied as the choice of administrators hired for the job.

For these and other reasons it is obvious that we do not have a system efficiently related to our alleged, often stated objectives of rehabilitating individuals to take their place as productive members of society. The myths of tradition, ignorance of human behavior, lack of central control and uniformity all contribute in their own way to dog the steps of increasingly complex social and economic relationships. Dr. Studt states appropriately— "When we analyze the social task currently assigned to the Correctional organization we find an uncoordinated collection of responsibilities, accumulated through a century and a half of Correctional operation and harboring serious potential conflicts among its goals."[38]

If we think in terms of the hodgepodge of uncoordinated agency goals that make up our Correctional process, we are naturally led to the seeking of a method for rational alignment. A reorganization of services may be a partial answer, but the question remains, who is to do it? Probably *only the community itself can produce coordination on this level.*

At certain periods of time crises situations of one type or another focus attention on Correctional problems and some agencies in a given community may temporarily work out systems and methods of cooperation and coordination. They usually revert back to their own previous defined operational goals, however. It is only when the community realigns its patterns of distribution and allocation of social and economic resources to a system which fits its own needs that any large degree of coordination is reached or assured.

In simpler terms, forces representing the community decide upon an administrative plan of procedure and proceed to implement it by reallocating the community's resources as a means of control. There is a certain amount of difficulty in applying the word community to any area. It is obvious that there are many uses of the term community ranging from a geographical entity to describing the object of a common interest. It is necessary here to use it as a collective term for referring to that grouping of individuals interacting within a given local environment producing a set of circumstances causing deviance by some from the social norms. Problems of delinquency are primarily local problems and must be approached locally.

[38] *Ibid.,* p. 9.

For *Correction* then, the *community becomes the client on a par with the individual. Skill in engaging the community becomes a necessary requirement of the Correctional agency.*

Several concepts need here to be clarified in order that we are not confused in our attempts to define the problem. The term "community organization" is variously defined. For social workers its central idea has been that it always starts and is developed in response to a community need as differentiated from an individual need. A given individual may signify it, but enough individuals are involved to affect the welfare of a given community. Therefore, the Correctional worker working with the personal community of a given individual client, while using some methods and techniques similar to those used in community organization, does not practice it, but merely *Correctional treatment strategy* with its constellation of skills selected according to individual case need.

One obviously does not engage a whole community. The engagement takes place through a mechanism, set up and selected by a given worker. This mechanism is a group or committee of individuals representing the community during the process of attempting change. The selection, engagement and management of the committee process requires skill and experience.

Correctional workers have not usually been trained in this skill nor has the organization of work loads permitted the devotion of much time to this area. However, even if he were trained, the average direct service worker in Corrections is not going to do much community organization as defined above unless specifically designated by his agency to do so.

The coordination of agency goals in any given system takes place at the administrative level only. It usually requires the presence of several factors.

It may be generally hypothesized that at least three conditions must be present before coordination can occur in any substantive amount: Agencies must have: (1) shared goals, (2) complementary resources, (3) efficient mechanisms for controlling whatever exchanges are involved.[39]

We are referring here not only to the skill of the initial plan-

[39] Reid, *op. cit.,* p. 421.

ning and the bringing about of an agreement on shared goals, but the maintenance of whatever control mechanisms are necessary to keep the exchanges operating in an efficient manner. Workers at the direct service level do not usually have authority to commit or speak for their agency in the exchange of resources. Agency administration only has the authority to make decisions for determining any sustained program involvement.

For systematic case coordination such control mechanisms may take the form of interagency agreements of regularly scheduled case conferences between staff members of different agencies. Program coordination may require such mechanisms as formal agreements, accountability procedures, interagency conferences and allocations of coordinating responsibilities *to specific staff members....*

If coordination control is at the practitioner or even supervisory level, policy issues cannot be resolved. Control operation must be expanded to include agency administration at various levels. Much the same may be said about program coordination. Not only are the activities likely to be highly complex and difficult to routinize, but control devices must often be expanded to involve total staff. . . . Such problems may be compounded when the agencies are large and heavily bureaucratic. Here coordination control must deal not only with an imposing agency array of department heads and specialists but also with the agency's own internal organizational problems.[40]

The points to be made are those noted strongly by Reid—that unmediated coordination is very difficult to achieve and that coordination may not necessarily be advantageous to the agencies involved, as they define their goals and functions. Thus the direct service worker in Corrections will not usually be equipped to effectively bring about and maintain effective agency coordination at a very involved level. The political and economic implications of coordination are many. Those who are skilled in the process are few.

E. Conclusion

If it is true that the family, the church and the neighborhood have a diminished effect as a means of social control, and the Juvenile Court is charged with the responsibility for the child's

[40] Reid, *op. cit.*, p. 426. (Emphasis added.)

welfare, the Court must provide leadership to the community to help develop effective substitutes or to redevelop family, neighborhood or citizen responsibility. Thus other agencies and institutions are brought into the process along with the community. If this is to be done efficiently, a means of organization for effective cooperation must be provided with a structure designed to permit achievement of the Court's objectives, and not necessarily those of participating agencies or institutions, which may be different.

The Court is in a particularly good position to see the gaps in services which exist in the community, to bring these gaps to the attention of planning groups in the community and to work with them to secure more adequate services. We can therefore summarize:

1. Juvenile Courts, along with other community agencies, have a responsibility for bringing about wholesome changes in the community.

2. This does not mean that the Court would take over planning in this area. It does mean that the Court would take an increased aggressive role in securing the resources it needs to do its job by planning with the community.

3. All types of political considerations are operative here. The Judge must be helped to see that in order for the Juvenile Court idea to be tried he must do all in his power, utilizing all the prestige of his position and status to obtain for the Court the cooperation and resources he needs to make it work.

The problem of juvenile delinquency is so complex that no one single cause for it can be said to exist. If we accept this, then it is logical to assume that no one single service for its prevention, treatment, and control is possible. The Juvenile Court cannot itself repair the defects and strains in the social order to which deviant behavior is a normal response. Nor can it provide the opportunity denied by a community. The problem is broadly and intricately based, interwoven into the very fabric of our culture.

It then is the community's obligation to change its attitude and structure when adequate and valid reasons are demonstrated for change. To the extent that some of the attitudes prevalent in the community need to change, we may speak of a necessary process of at least partial *community resocialization.*

Juvenile Correction law must then be thought of as a system and a process. That process is the uniting of law with the theories of human behavior to insure protection of the community and the individual. The system is made up of those agencies participating in the process. Factors necessary to its accomplishment are:

a. The exercising of a deliberate process of social control.

b. The utilization of the law to carry out an effective process of rehabilitation. These two functions are not separable. Not only must the law provide the necessary material and organizational resources for accomplishing this purpose, but the concepts of the law must connote rehabilitation and a strong social interest in the rights and future of the individual as an adequately functioning member of the community.

To understand adequately many of the aforementioned thoughts, the next chapter develops the theory on which they are based.

III. Some Theoretical Approaches: Application to the Task of Probation.

Peter O. Rompler

A. Introduction.

Delinquency is a failure to comply with norms. The question needs to be asked, whose norms were violated, and with or against whom did a youngster become delinquent? The offender cannot be viewed in isolation, without reference to his social environment. When we say that probation is a community effort, we mean that *the correctional effort, just as the causation of delinquency, is something that transcends the individual.* Even an individual-centered, clinically oriented treatment could not ignore the fact that a violation of the law had occurred because the offender's behavior conflicted with the norms of the larger society. Inasmuch as norms are an expression of culture, an individual's behavior, if governed by norms, is "cultural." In this respect, *personality is the individual manifestation of culture.*[1]

There may be a question of whether the value-systems within which offenders operate are consistent enough to warrant the statement that they in fact come from a "delinquent subculture." However, we do see the individual offender (as in fact all individuals) as Elliot Studt puts it, at "the nexus of a web of complex relationships." This implies that the web may be—or should become—the client.

This means that resocialization of the offender involves not

---

[1] "Personality," in this context, refers to those behaviors which people *share* with most others in their culture. Some writers refer to it therefore as *modal* personality.

only work with him personally, but requires a great deal of attention to the relationships between the offender and those important to him. The offender is seen not so much as the villain whose acting out against society is the only cause of concern, but rather as the person in whom defects in a faulty web of social relationships may have become manifest.

Before the action system of resocialization can become effective, communication needs to be established. That is to say, the worker as well as the elements of the "web" have to be sure they know what each is talking about, expecting, demanding, or driving at. Each participant in that process has to be able to put himself in the attitude of the other, to understand him in context.

Formulation of goals and realistic plans to achieve them will also have to be done with the "web" as client in mind. That is Elliot Studt's point when she writes that *resocialization involves change in both the individual and the system to which he belongs.*

Both the offender and his social environment, then, need to change for resocialization to become a fact. The offender operates under the additional handicap that some people in his environment may not only see in him the only one who is at fault for misbehaving but expect further violations of the law from him, i.e., label him as a "bad guy." Such a label may not only present an obstacle to a probationer's straightening out (e.g., through difficulties finding a job or being accepted back in school), but may also cause him to live up to the role thus assigned to him. Which is one way of saying that "individual" behavior is more than the consequence of individual rational choices.

Social workers, by and large, will agree to this, due to the attention they pay, especially during training, to the teachings of psychiatry. In these pages, however, we are going to explore another source of behavior, an area which also transcends individual rational decisions: the interrelatedness of individual behavior and the social matrix of which the actor is a part. It is the purpose of this chapter to clarify some of the elements of this approach. Who says that "personality is the individual manifestation of culture"? What are the consequences of such an idea for Corrections? What is meant by an "action system," a subculture, and who "puts himself in the attitude" of whom? Is an understanding of this important for our conception of the web of relationships, or for remedial action, or both?

To indicate our orientation in the in-service training phase of the 1964-65 probation training-demonstration project, we used the notion that *Corrections is a community effort*. The reasons for this are theoretical in nature. That is to say, propositions, some of them supported by empirical work, orientations, frames of reference for thought about social and cultural processes and structures, in short, statements concerning the interpretation of human phenomena from a variety of fields of knowledge have entered into our thinking with respect to the problems which probation officers face, and thus caused us to organize the particular kind of training effort that has occupied us recently.

The following is an exposé of the elements of our theoretical orientation, in which the concepts of culture, values, socialization, consciousness, action system, responsibility, the mission of corrections, and bureaucracy will be treated, and in that order. It is hoped that the outline of relevant theories will help to explain why we see community resocialization as the aim of Corrections and how a synthesis of theoretical elements from cultural anthropology, social psychology, and structural-functional analysis provided a framework for both the in-service training and the probation training phases of our project.

B. Elements of a Systematic Approach to the Study of the Genesis of Behavior and to Planned Remedial Action.

Culture. The popular meaning of this term, comprising motivation and skills in the arts, knowledge of the "finer" things in life, etc., does not concern us here. We are interested in culture as a guiding concept for the study of those human behaviors that are shared and traditional and may be reflected in things people make and use in traditional and commonly understood ways. Although formal definitions abound, few seem to have improved on that by Sir E. B. Tylor, given in 1874, who described culture as

. . . that complex whole which includes knowledge, belief, art, morals, law, custom, and any other capabilities and habits acquired by man as a member of society.[2]

Culture is universal in the sense that all people learn such a complex whole, which may be more or less consistent, stable or changing. Inasmuch as different populations, depending on their history, size, habitat, and relative isolation, develop *different complexes* of this sort, we speak of "cultures," and when the plural is used, the reference is to the particular modes of life of particular peoples. Complementing Tylor's definition, Herskovits writes:

All [cultures] have a philosophy of life, that is, a religious system. With song and dance and tale, the graphic and plastic art forms to give aesthetic satisfaction, language to convey ideas, and a system of sanctions and goals to give meaning and point to living, we round out this summary of these aspects of culture which, like culture as a whole, are attributes of all human groups.[3]

It is the contention of cultural anthropologists that all these "attributes" are linked together systematically, and that each of them must be studied and appreciated in context, i.e., in relation to all the others. Also important to remember are their historical continuity and the fact that the behaviors involved *are learned*. The learning, or the absorption, or internalization of all this is called socialization. Of particular interest to us is the learning of norms, or "values."

Values. For the purposes of this presentation it seems best to adopt the views of George Herbert Mead. He was a pragmatic philosopher and what might be called a behavioral social psychologist. He is also listed as a "symbolic interactionist," a term which will become clear later. To him,

. . . value is the character of an object in its capacity of satisfying an interest—*it resides neither in the object alone nor in an emotional state of the subject.*[4]

By "object" is meant an object of attention, which means not

---

[2] Tylor, Sir E. B., *Primitive Culture,* quoted here from Melville J. Herskovits, *Cultural Anthropology,* New York, Knopf, 1958, p. 305.

[3] Herskovits, *op. cit.,* p. 307.

[4] Charles W. Morris, Introduction to George H. Mead, *Mind, Self, and Society,* Chicago, University of Chicago Press, 1934, p. xxxi. (Emphasis added.)

necessarily anything material; the "neither-nor" clause indicates that value is nothing objectively "there," either outside or inside the interested party, but something that exists between the object and the subject, arising as it were in their interaction. A law, for example, whatever its abstract properties, becomes a value only as it satisfies somebody's interest. If it is against my interest, it would be a negative value to me, and I might be inclined to break it.[5] In the event that it neither satisfies nor obstructs any interest of mine, I would very likely be indifferent to it, and symbolic interactionism would thereby define it as *meaningless* to me.

Societies differ. There are differences not only in detail; not only specific attributes of culture vary from society to society, but also the degree to which these are integrated, mutually supportive, compatible or complementary. In small, traditional, isolated societies, there is a great degree of homogeneity: people look, act, and work pretty much alike. Therefore, their interests are similar, if not identical, so that any given object in the above sense is likely to be viewed by everybody in a similar fashion. The result is *high agreement on values*. Typically, values are not questioned in such societies, and alternatives are unknown or even inconceivable.

Our society, however, is large, heterogeneous, and changing at a fast pace. There is frequent and intensive contact between subgroups. Inasmuch as these subgroups have common interests (and therefore common values) within themselves, they may be said to have a subculture. It is evident that the moment people from reasonably different subgroups meet and have to deal with one another, there will be a clash of values. That is to say, individuals from different groups, being immersed in different cultures, will have different views of the same objects. The same law, to retain our example, will satisfy the interests of members of one group, but not necessarily those of another. They will therefore value it differently. This is not surprising once we realize that

[5] Whether a given object is valued positively or negatively by the knowing subject also depends on his perspective. Thus, I might deplore having to pay taxes, as they reduce my income. Yet when called upon to vote for a bond issue, my perspective becomes that of a responsible citizen, and I may be in favor of the issue.

a complex society may not have "a" culture, but many different and possibly conflicting ones that exist side by side or, in terms of their carriers, among one another.

A complex society is thus faced with the problem of making different value systems compatible, or establishing priorities and preferences. Standards need be developed and attempts at accommodation or assimilation made.

Assuming that this task is amenable to rational treatment, it is conceivable that individuals decide to pioneer a new and more workable value system. This may well be at variance with any of the systems existing at the time. Judgment of such an attempt has to take into consideration whether the individual in question is a rebel with or without a cause. If he has a cause, and he acts with a "higher" or "better" society in mind, he engages still in moral conduct. For these are its essentials to George Herbert Mead:

> . . . that there should be a social organization and that the individual should maintain himself. The method for taking into account all of those interests which make up society on the one hand and the individual on the other is the method of morality.[6]

Does that mean license for everybody? G. H. Mead's criterion for the justification of action is social again, and as such neither existentialist nor Platonic. In Morris' words:

> The right [act] is neither subjective caprice nor a timeless essence; its universality is a social universality.[7]

Mead's definition of value allows the conception of personally, idiosyncratically held values. For these to become justifiable from the point of view of society, however, it is necessary that they do not conflict with universal values. We have seen before that cultural behaviors are shared and learned. That raises the question, what is the process by which culture is transmitted, including norms? Implied in that query is, of course, the obverse: how is it that some people do not come to live by the norms "universal" in their society?

---

[6] G. H. Mead, *op. cit.*, p. 389.
[7] Morris, in G. H. Mead, *op. cit.*, p. xxxiii.

According to Arthur Miles, our administration of justice regards most offenders as wrong, not sick.[8] In view of what we have said above, that implies non-compliance with universal values on the side of the offender. How does one learn to comply?

Socialization.

The Freudian psychologist, concentrating on the mechanisms within the individual, was the first to give a working account of the way in which children, born into Euro-American bourgois culture of the last fifty years, took on that culture. This was not, of course, the way in which they phrased their accomplishment.[9]

Of course they did not phrase it that way. For what they found they assumed to be universally applicable. The process of socialization as studied by this school was largely taken as inherent in human nature itself. The central feature of this process was superego formation which involves the generalization and gradual abstraction of parental authority. As the dicta of father or mother or whoever played their role are internalized, *guilt* takes the place of the physically restraining force of the parent.

What Margaret Mead was leading up to in the above quotation, is the uncovering of two, as it has turned out, erroneous assumptions: (1) that superego formation and the development of guilt as internalized control is the universal way of socializing humans and (2) that the transmission of culture always involves the child becoming like his parents. The first of these assumptions she disproves by describing three primitive societies she studied (the Balinese, the Iatmul of New Guinea, and the Samoans); for the deflation of the second assumption she turns to our own society.

Seen within this cross-cultural perspective, our own superego system of character formation appears as a special and rather complicated development. . . Our system might work quite smoothly in a stable culture. . . An essential element in the system is that the child is expected to become

[8] Arthur P. Miles, "The Reality of the Probation Officer's Dilemma," *Federal Probation*, Vol. 29, No. 1 (March, 1965), p. 21.

[9] Margaret Mead, "Social Change and Cultural Surrogates," *Journal of Educational Sociology*, Vol. 14 (1940), pp. 92-110. This quotation is from the reprint in Clyde Kluckhohn and Henry A. Murray, *Personality in Nature, Society and Culture*, New York, Knopf, 1948, p. 512.

like the parent . . . to take the parent as a model for his own life style. *In periods of rapid change,* and especially when these are accompanied by migrations and political revolutions, *this requirement of the system is unattainable.*

. . . when a world in which the children already live is a different world from that in which their parents grew up and when the world in which they will be adults will have still a different pattern, the socializing function of the *age group* becomes very much intensified. . . The majority of young people respond eagerly to the approval and shrink away from the disapproval of their age mates.[10]

It should be noted that the *age group* rather than, say, a model individual, appears as a parent surrogate with respect to controls. Perhaps the constant presence in today's youth of fads and crazes is intelligible in these terms. Conformance to an ever-changing youth culture takes the place of growing up into the adult role on the parental model. Inasmuch as this shift has been largely incomplete, parents continue to be models, accepted reluctantly perhaps and to varying degrees. If in this situation of dual orientation (i.e., attempts at compliance with both the personal, partly outmoded norms instilled by parents and the collective, up-to-date but shifting norms of the peer group) serious discrepancies appear between the two sets of values, an internal conflict or an adaptive "compartmentalization" may be the result.

In a critical examination of the utilitarian theory of social action which is described as overly rationalistic, Talcott Parsons observes that *ritual actions* have become ". . . the most prominent class of concrete actions thus overlooked."[11] The sociologically significant fact about ritual is the function it has for the participants. It serves to perpetuate social cohesion, may give the individual reconfirmed status and a "sense of belonging," keeping his rights and obligations in focus. In the case of primitive societies, ritual is compulsive. We have seen from Margaret Mead's observations that in many non-Western societies there is no internalization of

---

[10] *Ibid.,* quoted from Kluckhohn and Murray, *op. cit.,* pp. 518-519. Cf. also Talcott Parsons, "Age and Sex in the Social Structure of the United States," *American Sociological Review,* Vol. 7 (1942), pp. 604-616; reprinted in Kluckhohn and Murray, *op. cit.,* pp. 269-281. (Emphasis added.)

[11] Talcott Parsons, *The Structure of Social Action,* Glencoe, Free Press, 1949, p. 57.

authority in the form of guilt. Instead, there are the external sanctions of the group, demanding compliance. One of the important differences between preliterate, traditional societies and complex ones such as our own is the repressive and retributive nature of primitive law of the former as contrasted with the restitutive, remedial tendency in our own legal system.

Perhaps we should take a clue from the utilitarian oversight as pointed out by Parsons. Suppose a youngster acts mostly in compliance with peer group norms which, as we have seen, he does not internalize but knows to be compelling as long as he wishes to remain in the group. How likely is it that he will accept the probation officer as a model? If he has an inadequately developed superego, that will be difficult. But even if his "conscience" is fairly developed, the conflicting repressive norms of his reference group may keep him in a state of very uneasy suspension.

Acting tough, joy-riding, shop-lifting, etc., are not always activities engaged in "for kicks," but have to be done for the youngster to have status with his peers. The ritual nature of transgression, if it be that, all but precludes successful work with the offender alone and, incidentally, makes even the inclusion of the family (e.g., parents) an insufficient tactical device.

All of this suggests that a theory of socialization which regards the family as the primary transmitter of cultural norms is a postulate rather than a fair description of existing conditions. Parents *may* be the main agents of the transmittal. If so, an offender probably has much in common, as far as conscience goes, with middle class people (e.g., his probation officer), because the transmittal of culture through parents is the mode of socialization practiced by the middle classes. Prospects for treatment will tend to be good. But to assume the *universal* validity of the superego—formation-via-the-family thesis is naïve at best and counter to the evidence. If it is adhered to in the training of correctional personnel, it is grotesque and irresponsible, because it fails to prepare the trainee for those cases in which something other than middle-class attempts at socialization is necessary.

Culture, then, has many faces and a variety of metabolisms. Not only the contents, or attributes vary, but also the modes of their perpetuation, which is important to us because of the heterogeneity of our own society.

We have mentioned the superego, or conscience, and contrasted other modes of behavior control with its operation. We have also seen how the same objects may satisfy different interests in different people and are then "valued" differently, which precludes the notion of an "objective" environment. This is of interest to correctional personnel in view of the argument that much rehabilitative effort is undone by leaving a probationer in the environment that helped produce his delinquency in the first place: His *subjective* environment may in fact have been changed through treatment. On the other hand, it would have been changed only for him, and in a fashion that pays no attention to relapses based on a possible reversal to his former mode of perceiving and thinking. For a modified value system to be stabilized, supervision has to work on both the client and his significant others.

It is well at this point to expand our discussion of the position which the individual occupies vis-à-vis society. Who is the client in corrections in his capacity as a perceiving, thinking, responding human being? What does our pragmatic-behaviorist view, adopted from George Herbert Mead, have to offer by way of explaining the postulated need for including significant others in the process of probation? What is it that suggests the conception of the client as being more than the individual who comes to the office for his appointment?

We want to raise the question, what are the processes by which humans see the world? How are things and people recognized and thought about? It is this area to which we will turn next.

Consciousness. We are returning to symbolic interactionism, already mentioned and described as a behavioristic social psychology. Because of its pragmatic base, its avoidance of constructs which are difficult to treat empirically, it is particularly well adapted to give sense and guidance to practice.

First of all, this school of thought does not conceive of nature and everything in it as "out there," objectively, whereas my consciousness, the knowing subject's faculties are "in here," inside my cranium. Commenting that the system-forming periods were hardly yet in evidence (1934), Morris observes that George Herbert Mead's social psychology (and probably his whole philosophy, for that matter; P. R.) is

> . . . a naturalism which sees thinking man *in* nature, and which aims to avoid the inherited dualisms of mind and matter, experience and nature, philosophy and science . . . theory and practice.[12]

The individual does not behold nature, he participates in it. How can he be aware of it? Through the self:

> The self is not so much a substance as a process in which *the conversation of gestures has been internalized* within an organic form. This process does not exist for itself, but is simply a phase of the whole social organization of which the individual is a part.[13]

The notion of consciousness as a participation in nature will be better understood when Mead's concept of "mind" is introduced. In Morris' words:

> Mind is the presence in behavior of significant symbols. It is the internalization within the individual of the social process of communication in which meaning emerges.[14]

Unlike the Freudian concept of the ego, which is to be comprehended as an intrinsic property of the individual, G. H. Mead's concept of "mind" is a process *between* people. In his view, conversation is an exchange of gestures, i.e., significant symbols. For these to have meaning, the communicating individuals have to put themselves into each other's attitude. To make myself understood, I have to listen to myself as I imagine my partner to be listening. For a comment, a "verbal gesture" to be understood, alter's response has to be anticipated with a reasonable amount of accuracy. Hence the definition of a symbol as ". . . a stimulus whose response is given in advance. . ."[15] If the response is "given" incorrectly (i.e., wrongly anticipated), communication will not occur, and the gesture is a meaningless stimulus. Note that this would not be anybody's "fault." The conception of meaning and

---

12 Charles Morris, in Mead, *op. cit.,* p. x. (Emphasis added.)
13 George H. Mead, *op. cit.,* p. 178. (Emphasis added.)
14 Charles Morris, in G. H. Mead, *op. cit,* p. xxii.
15 George H. Mead, *op. cit.,* p. 181.

communication discussed here would not permit a statement to the effect that if you do not understand me, that's your problem. It's *ours*.

What has been explained here with respect to the discourse between individuals can be expanded to explain the role of thinking man in nature. Objects in the world are beautiful, pleasant, dangerous or painful only because of the relationship between them and us. Organic forms (e.g., men) develop in a significant environment, i.e., ascribe value to the phenomena within it, and both influence each other. *The elements of mutual transformation constitute the field of consciousness.*[16]

Consciousness is thus indirectly defined, not as a spiritual, ethereal of otherwise abstract property, but behavioristically as the process in which objects, animate or inanimate, become meaningful to the subject. The question of cause and effect is not raised, nor need it be.

This process has certain logically antecedent elements, or "necessary conditions": distinguishable properties of the objects and the sensory apparatus of the subject. However, these elements are not simply the components of consciousness. This process is not reducible to any elements, it is a phenomenon *sui generis,* as it were, and *intrinsic not to an individual, but to a relationship between him and the external world.*

If this frame of reference is acceptable, the concept of "community resocialization" can be viewed in perspective. Elliot Studt pointed out that not only a probationer, but the complex web of faulty social relationships needs our attention. In the light of Mead's theory, we could hardly think otherwise. If "mind" and consciousness are entities inseparable from communication with others, if the "me" is the totality of internalized attitudes of significant others, any but the most superficial attempt at behavior change will have to take all the significant others, more precisely, the patterns of interaction with those others, into consideration. G. H. Mead comments on the position of the individual in the community:

One must take the attitude of the others in a group in order to belong

[16] George H. Mead, *op. cit.,* p. 330.

to a community. . . It is through his relationship to others that he has being as a citizen.[17]

If becoming a citizen is one of the aims of socialization, and one to which corrections people pay special attention, then those relationships must be the focus of attention. Furthermore, if our concern about the inadequacy of familial relationships in modern, complex, fast changing societies is justified, the conclusion is unavoidable that the community at large must be the target of correctional efforts.

Action System. Common sense suggests that if something as complex as a community or a whole society is to be influenced in any way, the means to that end will have to be complex, too. For a first illumination of that aspect of our problem some of Talcott Parsons' reflections may be helpful. In his *Structure of Social Action* he identifies the "unit act" as the element of action and enumerates the following as necessary for an act to take place: (1) an agent (or "actor"); (2) an end (or "purpose"), i.e., a condition that is either different from the present but would not obtain without action being taken or, conversely, is equal to the present but would not endure without action; (3) the "situation"; that is a cluster of elements of the field of action, comprising two subcategories: (a) elements over which the actor has no control ("conditions"), and (b) elements over which he does have control ("means"); (4) a normative orientation: Since the choice of means is usually neither random nor fully determined by the conditions, the actor needs guidelines he can use to decide on the action to be taken.

The utilitarian theory of social action seems not to have recognized the last point. Parsons charges that theory with being naïvely empiricist[18] in that it assumed a rational action system to be composed of a mere aggregate of rational unit acts. Parallel with this idea went the atomistic notion that the actor was an aggregate unit, something doubtlessly inspired by the individualism of the last century.

What needs to take its place is the expectation, so to speak,

17 *Ibid.,* p. 199.
18 Parsons, *op. cit.,* p. 59.

a readiness to recognize that after end A (of the unit act A) has been achieved, the situation (possible means as well as conditions) for acts B, C . . . N has been altered. More simply: Any act within an action system must be expected to have reverberations throughout the system.

Example: Casework with an aggressive probationer, consisting as it does of a series of probationary unit acts, if successful, will not only alter the youngster's behavior, but have consequences for his relationships with parents and peers. That having occurred, the probationer, his parents, peers, and the probation officer will find the situation for all further acts changed.

This sounds so plausible, it is almost trite. The reader is referred to the Appendix, however, for an illustration of how easily just this feature of an action system may be overlooked (pp. 102-103) especially when there are agents in the system whose acts are not highly visible.

A change in the situation as a consequence of an act can, of course, be assessed and taken into consideration for further acts only if there is feedback, i.e., a way of learning about the degree to which the end of the unit act (or a series of them) has been achieved.

How far social action will have to go before it could be said to be in line with theory and research, can be seen at the discrepancy in sophistication between the theories just discussed (published 1934 and 1949, respectively) and an article on the theory of interagency coordination of December 1964.[19] In the latter, the author lists three levels of coordination: (1) *ad hoc* case coordination (one worker asking another for help, as a case comes up); (2) systematic case coordination ("service integration"[20]); routine interagency work, but still in behalf of individual clients; and (3) program coordination.[21] In the latter, coordination centers not about individual clients, but agency programs.

[19] William Reid, "Interagency Co-ordination in Delinquency Prevention and Control," *Social Service Review*, Vol. XXXVIII, No. 4 (Deember, 1964), pp. 418-428.
[20] So called by Alfred Kahn, *Planning Community Services for Children in Trouble*, New York, Columbia University Press, 1963, pp. 110-112, quoted by Reid, *op. cit.*, p. 420.
[21] Reid, *op. cit.*, p. 420.

Only the last of these three can properly be called an application of action system theory. For (1) and (2) are relatively simple theoretical structures, always joining all unit acts in one "end": the rehabilitation of *a* client. Program coordination, however, is much more sophisticated insofar as the action is planned without prior knowledge of who exactly the clients will be and how they will respond. Although in the light of Parsons' theory, the necessity of *ongoing* coordination with the help of information from the field through an established feedback mechanism seems clearly indicated, this is not acknowledged. Not even the dynamic nature of an agency-supersystem becomes clear, leaving the treatment open to the criticism Parsons leveled against the utilitarian theorists: that of naïve empiricism.

Even this much is almost more than we can hope for at existing levels of organization for welfare. Too often, as Reid indicates, agencies achieve "insular self-sufficiency"[22] by defining the range of problems to be treated in terms of the resources available to them. Executives of such agencies may consider themselves eminently practical and efficient. Meanwhile, any client with a problem which existing agencies do not happen to be equipped for is out of luck.

One aspect of the "naïve empiricism" which still pervades our institutions is the absence of any norm covering social tasks whose accomplishment requires the use of complex resources and sophisticated organization. Given the size and complexity of these tasks, the government, national, state, or local, looks like a likely candidate for assuming such an obligation. But with the exception of the defense establishment and the Office of Economic Opportunity, no effective large-scale social action systems seem to have been developed.

Is that anybody's fault? Who is responsible for what remains undone?

Responsibility. Let me first state what I do *not* mean by responsibility. I am not speaking about some character trait which, when you don't have it, makes you an irresponsible person. And I am not using the term as synonymous with "obligation."

---

[22] Reid, *op. cit.,* p. 424.

I like to think of responsibility as a vector *sui generis,* namely, as *the degree to which and the direction in which people operating in a social system are accountable for their actions.*

I will explain "direction" first: responsibility goes in the direction from where authority (i.e., *legitimate* power) comes. Any agent, individual or collective, is responsible, that is, accountable for his or their actions, to the person or the agency that delegates authority to them. This alone makes it obvious that the notion of responsibility as entertained here cannot be connected just with individuals, any more than can conscience or mind in Mead's scheme.

With respect to the degree of responsibility we may expect in a social system, we will only be able to raise a few disturbing questions. Durkheim speaks of anomic societies as those in which effective norms for conduct are absent. A society in which this is literally true is hard to conceive, but anomie may be considered a variable, and then we can offer the proposition that *the greater the degree of anomie in a social system, the less accountable for their actions are the people operating within it.*

It seems that it would not make too much difference, whether anomie is literally the absence of norms or the result of their being mutually contradictory, as *is conceivable* in a heterogeneous society such as our own.

Also, *responsibility varies directly with authority.*

Only a person who has a legitimate choice of action can be held responsible. For example, whatever else incarceration may be expected to do for offenders, responsible in a social sense they cannot be while behind bars.

Let us apply the logic of this argument to the question raised above, namely, whose "fault" is it that existing actions or service systems are so fragmented? It appears that responsibility for the formation of complex action systems working in an integrated manner can be assigned only if someone is given both the power and the right, i.e., a *mandate,* to create such a system. That may become a working reality soon, but it has not been so in the past.

The Corrections Mission. According to Arthur Miles, probation officers in Wisconsin reject the usual assumptions of casework.[23] Perhaps that is as it should be, not because those assumptions are all wrong, but because with respect to the total problem posed to the field of corrections they are beside the point. The foregoing pages hopefully helped to make clear why.

Ours is a complex society, with great heterogeneity of values which means that some of the value systems operating in our society are conflicting, reducing one another's effectiveness. Values recognized as binding by the "official" society, but not shared by members outside the dominant strata whose value systems underlie the law of the land, will be meaningless to those non-participants in the dominant culture. Besides, even such common values as do persist are not transmitted to the young equally in all subgroups, and not in the same manner. That means, among offenders from different cultural subgroups we may expect to find different modal personalities, not to mention the fact that most of them will be very different from the workers who have contact with them.

Since different personalities require different treatment, approaches must be variable. Personality was seen as the individual manifestation of culture. That may mean that unless mass deportation and cultural up-rooting of delinquent or pre-delinquent individuals is considered feasible, the cultures which support them, or, to get closer to Margaret Mead's conception, which is their mechanism of control, may have to be changed *in toto*.

Obviously, such a task is beyond the individual worker, and also beyond individual agencies. The logic of symbolic interactionism is very neatly translatable into a discussion of agency functions. The socialization of the community cannot be done *by* agencies *to* the community, but by communities as a whole, with the agencies playing an integral part.

The role of the law in this process has been elucidated somewhat in the previous chapter. What the leadership function of the Courts will look like or the contribution of lawyers in particular, I cannot say. At the moment, it seems that their roles converge

[23] Miles, *op. cit.*, p. 2.

very much with those of correctional workers. As Talcott Parsons observes:

> [The lawyer] stands as a kind of buffer between the illegitimate desires of his client and the social interest.[24]

As other professionals, he is interested in reducing deviance, in his case, deviation from the law. At the same time, he must retain the confidence of his clients. In this respect, his work is very much comparable to that of the social worker in Corrections.

In summary we can say, then, that the "mission" of Corrections comprises behavioral change in offenders, such as to bring their actions within the limits permissible by law; that this involves a relearning of values in individual offenders, and, inasmuch as their values are rooted in faulty relationships with others or in deviant subcultures from which they come, the restoration of such relationships or a modification of part of a community with respect to norms, in other words, *community resocialization*.

Bureaucracy. Services may be institutionalized through the development of appropriate, administered organizations. Ideally, this increases efficiency: roles (and "plot") are defined, and there is an alignment of facilities and talent with need, or with the tasks that appear.

It would be a mistake, however, to confuse this *intended* rational alignment with the actual development of bureaucratic structures. Through the processes discussed by G. H. Mead, not only do individuals take up roles (as objects) in an administrative function, but they in turn are absorbed by their roles and become bureaucrats. I suspect something like this to be the explanation for the fact, reported by Miles, that trained and untrained workers, after several years of service, function in about the same way.[25] This phenomenon seems to be repeated, in a negative way, in the practically traditional reluctance of social welfare agencies other than the Court to work with offenders. Harvey Treger writes to this point,[26] listing the following observations: Social agencies

---

[24] Talcott Parsons, "A Sociologist Looks at the Legal Profession" in *Essays in Sociological Theory*, Glencoe, Free Press, 1954, p. 384.

[25] Miles, *op. cit.*, p. 21.

[26] Harvey Treger, "Reluctance of the Social Agency to Work with the Offender," *Federal Probation*, Vol. 29, No. 1 (March, 1965), pp. 23-28.

feel uncomfortable working with the Courts; agency workers tend to project their own lack of motivation to work with offenders on them, labeling them as "not motivated" to be treated; agency workers, like their clients, seek a comfortable level of operation:

> Many workers prefer to work with people who have more intra-psychic problems. *They view this as a higher, more professional type of work*.[27]

It is very improbable that the characteristics of agencies and attitudes of workers described here are due to rational choices on the side of the workers. We may suspect that all these symptoms of reluctance to work with offenders find a higher level explanation if we consider the workers as *institutionally constrained,* socialized into a system with its own traditions, and operating in an organization which has an institutional life of its own, irrespective of its original purpose. Its personnel will develop views, attitudes, and habits in line with this. We could call it professional ethnocentrism, or plain parochialism. What I do, in my office, is right and normal. Work with people outside my realm is odd, unhealthy, lower status and to be avoided.

C. Problems Calling For a Systematic Approach: The Organization of Corrections.

In the preceding section, we have listed some theoretical elements of a systematic approach as we describe it here. That effort itself had a system to it. Consider the list of elements in vertical arrangement:

Culture
Values
Socialization
Consciousness

*

Action system
Responsibility
The task of corrections
Bureaucracy

[27] *Ibid.,* p. 24. (Emphasis added.)

While listing the problems calling for a systematic approach to the organization of corrections, we can sum up what has so far been said, picking these concepts one by one, starting at the asterisk:

(1) *Consciousness is a process* by which things and people, their shapes, movements, tastes, laws, caprices and predictabilities become meaningful to the subject. This process is shared with others, through the mediating function of the mind; the development of a set of internalized attitudes of others (producing, through communication, shared understandings) is the core of *socialization*. We want to pay special attention to the emergence of those common perceptions that are of consequence to the satisfaction of the subject's interests: the characteristics of objects called *values*. The totality of common understandings, perceptions and "valuations" as well as the human activities designed to perpetuate and transmit these, such as the establishment of social institutions, the observance of rituals (religious as well as temporal) and the traditional practices of child rearing, make up, and are at the same time controlled by, *culture*.

(2) *The mutuality of the processes* which constitute culture, socialization, consciousness and motivation, the complexity of multilateral transformations, the way in which events are causes and effects at the same time, is of the essence of an *action system*. We can view this as a theory, i.e., as a frame of reference, a way of explaining the phenomenal world. But we can also see in it a model for the construction of a set of coordinated activities, designed to achieve specified results. Inasmuch as we are concerned with the protection, improvement or re-creation of a society in which certain specified conditions obtain, participants in the social system (which, as we have seen, is a process, not a static structure) must be accountable for their actions. This feature we call *responsibility*. The construction and maintenance of those conditions which make a high degree of responsibility probable is *the task of Corrections*. Its magnitude and complexity have led to the development of large organized institutional structures whose character as *bureaucracies* calls our attention to both

their virtues and their faults: potential efficiency and a potentially calcified state of affairs in which the inner life of the establishment rather than its purpose dictates its function.

Why should we be interested in organized activities so large that their inner workings might render them ineffective, so complex that their mere comprehension, let alone control, becomes problematical, so sophisticated that the cost of their administration threatens to be prohibitive?

The answer has to do with the complexity of our society. We are interested in the reduction or, if possible, prevention, of delinquency. It seems logical to look for the cause or causes of delinquency and then work on these. Let me point out a flaw in that reasoning: "Delinquency" is not, strictly speaking, a form of conduct, but the absence of one. *Delinquere* (Latin) means to fail. Now it stands to reason that the "causes" of something that fails to occur will be difficult to discover. Being less abstract and philosophical about it, we may observe that the large variety of delinquent behaviors cannot possibly be explained by a common cause or even a cluster of causes. Truancy, drinking by minors, assault, shoplifting and gang warfare are all against the law, but that is about where their commonality ends. If we wish to learn why some people fail to abide by the law, we will have to look for the reasons for that failure in the process of socialization, and that is complex. Within any one culture, it is complex, and much more so in a heterogeneous society like ours.

(3) *Cultural Differentiation.* A complex society is characterized, among other things, by a high division of labor. People are specialized. Specialties are grouped together, some by the criterion of purpose, some by degree of necessary training. It may be the latter criterion that accounts for the different prestige enjoyed by the various occupational or professional groups. Whatever its origin, there exists in modern society a system of stratification, a hierarchical order of classes, whose best indicator is the occupations of their members.

Not only their occupations differ, however, but also their styles of life, their tastes, their interests, their possessions (in quality as well as in quantity), and their philosophy of life. It is an illusion that all of us think and act pretty much the same.

When people of diverse social backgrounds are brought together, they may have difficulty talking; they may feel uneasy, out of place; or they may offend one another, or feel that they have "nothing in common." This latter notion is also an illusion. The truth is that the farther apart on the social status ladder people are, the more difficult it may be for them to establish "common ground."

That includes their view on law and morals. The difference between a middle class and a lower class person is not that the former person "has" morals and the latter does not, but that the middle class person's morality is much more likely to be reflected in law than that of members of the lower strata. Consequently, the latter neither see nor care to look for any beauty in the law, or for rousing sentiment because of its tradition, or for comfort because it makes and keeps things right. Law to them may be something that people use to evict them, to take things away from them, or that helps put them behind bars.

These are but illustrations. The point is that life style, perception and value systems *vary*. They are *different in kind* in different classes and ethnic groups, not only different in degree.[28]

Moreover, not only the contents of the value systems differ, but also the way they are organized and transmitted, as indicated before. Cultural discrepancies are liable to be sharpened by the fact that cultural change may take place at *uneven rates* in different groups, especially if they are socially isolated, not participating in an adequate "roof culture" (a poor term of mine for what might otherwise be called the culture of a social supersystem).

Our trouble, then, has to do with value—heterogeneity in time and place, with occupational, class, regional and ethnic variation,

---

[28] For a pertinent illustration of this, see the description of lower class sex mores by William Foote Whyte, "A Slum Sex Code," *American Journal of Sociology*, Vol. 49 (July, 1943), pp. 24-31; reprinted in Reinhard Bendix and Seymour Martin Lipset, *Class, Status and Power*, Glencoe, Free Press, 1953, pp. 308-316.

For a more comprehensive treatment of class differences with respect to values, see Herbert H. Hyman, "The Value Systems of Different Classes: A Social-Psychological Contribution to the Analysis of Stratification," R. Bendix and S. M. Lipset, *op. cit.*, pp. 426-342. This article offers a wealth of empirical data.

all of which could be complementary and compatible, but evidently aren't. There is a clash of values, goals, and philosophy.

If the correctional worker uses himself as a therapeutic tool, and if there is an important difference between his own sociocultural background and that of his clients, he is a stranger in more ways than one to the very people with whom he is expected to work.

(4) *Suboptimization in Corrections and the Situation of the Practitioner.* The detrimental or at least ineffectual nature of professional ethnocentrism or parochialism stems not so much from the fact that the practitioner may hold values different from those of his clients, but from the assumption that enlightenment of the client, a sort of transfer of knowledge or "insight," is what is needed. Values are not wares, commodities that can be shifted and rearranged at will. They operate in complex, more or less consistent systems. Delinquency was defined above as a failure to comply with norms. It is important to note that *the criterion of compliance is ours, not necessarily that of the offender.* He may well have acted within the framework of values that is meaningful to him. If that framework is socially unacceptable, it has to be changed. But that involves more than the offender and may be a task too big for the worker.

The capabilities of the individual officer are obviously limited. However, he may be more restricted than he needs to be. As long as he is trained to optimal performance without his efforts being integrated into a larger operating whole, part of his work and his preparation for it are lost to the correctional supersystem. This is called *suboptimization.*

(5) *The Court.* Social and cultural change will necessitate adjustment of correctional strategies, as the needs for intervention change. This may or may not involve changes on the case level. In any event, it must be guided by an agency with a bird's eye view. As long as correctional practitioners are employed by the Court and the public considers the Court the logical center from which correctional efforts are organized, it must assume the function of educator of its workers as well as the public (for reasons evident from Section A in this chapter) and see to it that

available resources are used appropriately (e.g., that workers do the work for which they are trained, unhampered by clerical chores, and on those clients who will benefit most from it).

IV. Synthesis: The Socio-Cultural Perspective, Generic Social Work And Corrections.

Peter O. Rompler

A. Introduction.

In the following chapter an attempt is made to work toward a definition of Corrections as that part of the welfare service system that aims at reduction and control of criminal and delinquent behavior in individuals and seeks to identify and abolish social and cultural conditions which encourage, induce or tolerate such behavior. Such a service system is seen as part of a complicated matrix of problems, tasks and actions. Generally, the discussion implies the logic of Elliot Studt's description of the *field of practice* within which correctional work takes place:

Thus any particular field of practice can be conceptualized as a *flow of human activities* among multiple representatives of the community, those individuals whose behavior is symptomatic of a certain social problem, and the organizations authorized to do something about the problem. The dynamic processes thus set in motion are ostensibly designed to change the people whose behavior evidences the particular social problem; actually they instigate changes in all the systems affected by and affecting the problem.[1] This flow of human activity, identifiable because it is focused on a particular social problem, is the relevant social environment within which the social work practice unit acts and from which it derives its field of practice characteristics.

However, social work practice is not just passively shaped by its par-

[1] Kenneth D. Benne, "Deliberate Changing as the Facilitation of Growth," *The Planning of Change* (New York: Holt, Rinehart, and Winston, 1961), pp. 230-234, quoted in Elliot Studt, *A Conceptual Approach to Teaching Materials* (New York: Council on Social Work Education, March, 1965), p. 16.

ticipation in its service-relevant environment. As one of the active components in a dynamic process, social work shares in shaping the field of practice even as it is affected by it. The analysis of a field of practice is useful not only for understanding the various adaptations required of social work as it participates with others in addressing one social problem or another. It also identifies the critical points in any service process where action for change will be most effective in improving service. Adaptation achieved by creative struggles with particular social realities should enrich our theoretical formulations and strengthen the profession whose competence lies in resolving problems of social functioning through service.[2]

Figure 1 on page 61 gives an idea what the correctional system comprises and how it relates to the total community. Strictly speaking, the three large circles in the diagram should occupy the same space. Since "The Problem," "The Task," and "The Service System" have to be displayed separately, the arrows between them are to indicate their interrelatedness. Solid-line arrows show the direction of action; broken arrows stand for the direction of information flow. This is to draw attention to the necessity of feedback, i.e., the results of action, in recognition of the dynamic nature of systematic planning. It is not to say that transmittal of information is essentially different from "action." In fact, such a distinction would be difficult to make in consideration of the more specific interaction between the components of the service system. Here, the arrows are all solid, but they, too, go in both directions. The "Problem" circle is drawn in a broken line to indicate the fact that crime and delinquency are part of the life of the total community and open to influences coming from it (e.g., economic changes, urban renewal programs, political changes resulting in different modes of law enforcement, population movements, etc.).

The three sections within the "Task" circle overlap, indicating that the subtasks they stand for are not separate. Rehabilitation of individual offenders obviously has significance for the safety of the community; such rehabilitation may be possible only, and certainly becomes more probable, as the community as a whole can be organized to help, e.g., by providing support for, and

[2] Studt, *op. cit.*, pp. 16-18.

TOTAL COMMUNITY

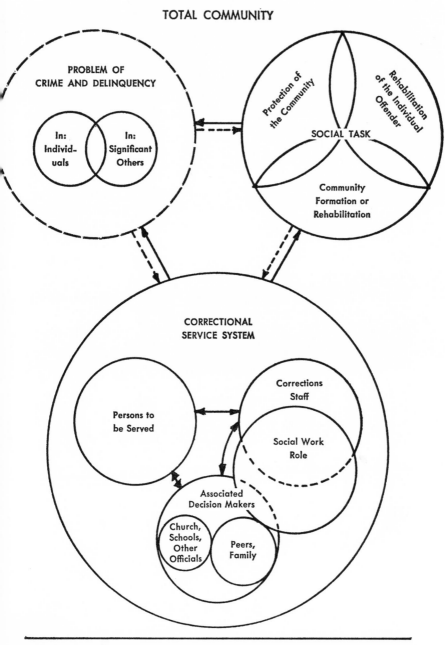

Figure 1: The Correctional Field of Practice. Adapted from: E. Studt, *op. cit.*, p. 17, with the permission of author and publisher.

restraints on, the probationer consistent with the effort by professionals within the correctional system.

The role of the social worker is shown as covering parts of the correctional staff as well as part of the area of associated decision-making. This should not be understood to mean that any individual worker would at the same time be filling positions within and outside a correctional agency. "Social Worker" is a generic term here. We find "the social worker" in probation and parole departments as well as in school systems as pupil welfare workers, in welfare agencies supported by churches, and many other agencies which at one time or another might be called upon for help in individual cases, or whose work is relevant as part of the milieu in which the task of corrections progresses.

Notice, too, that the Correctional Service System, as conceived here, includes as components not only professionals and professional institutions, but also peers and family (among "Associated Decision-Makers"). The inclusion of these is what the phrase "Community Formation" (as part of the Social Task) refers to: the development of systematic participation of community members other than professionals in the problem-solving process. This notion is a translation into social-system terms of a commonly accepted goal of casework, namely the strengthening of the client's self-reliance, resourcefulness and problem solving ability. The size of the circles in the diagram connotes the differential specificity of purpose, privacy of the target group, etc. It does not imply a judgment on the relative "importance" of the subsystems or components, or of the relative contribution to the solution of social problems. Since such a solution is seen as coming from a systematic, interactive effort, the ascription of certain proportions of the total contribution to elements of the system would be pointless.

In our Probation Training—Demonstration Project[3] we tried to translate some of this thinking into action. In one phase of the project, a group of second-year social work students who had their field placements with the St. Louis City Juvenile Court

[3] Institute for Delinquency Control, St. Louis University School of Social Service; funded by the President's Committee on Juvenile Delinquency and Youth Crime, under Grant No. 7:JD 62225.

were stationed as a unit within the demonstration area. That arrangement facilitated contact with their clients and their families. Supervision made use of casework as well as group work methods. The latter provided an opportunity to involve certain neighborhood centers in their efforts at the same time that probationers were made aware of existing facilities where they might turn for help or recreation later. Moreover, people in the neighborhood came to the unit supervisor with many problems, some of them quite unrelated to corrections, in which cases they were referred to appropriate sources of help. In short, the correctional system as represented by that branch office of the Juvenile Court became "permeable" at the same time that the student probation officers went about the task of involving formal and informal community resources (schools, churches, settlement houses, families) in their work.[4] Three features, based on the conceptual framework outlined in this essay, stand out: (1) flexibility of method, (2) recognition of the complex genesis of delinquent behavior and, consequently, (3) an attempt to avoid reliance on the one-to-one working relationship between worker and probationer.

The other phase of the Project has been in-service training, comprising summer institutes and monthly follow-up workshops for juvenile correctional officers and related personnel already in the field. In 1963, the emphasis was on diagnosis and treatment. In 1964 to 1965, attention was given to the study of resources outside the court. In the workshops of the 1964 summer institute particularly, there was much exchange of experience concerning ways in which such outside resources can be mobilized. Moreover, workshop participants showed not only considerable knowledge of existing resources, but were responsive to the need of comprehending them as a *system* composed of subsystems and individual workers within these whose actions are at least partly determined by the role they play within the institutional structure of which they are a part.

---

[4] A fuller account of this effort is given by the field instructor of that unit: Gerald M. Holden, *An Attempt at Training and Demonstration in Juvenile Probation.* Paper presented at the 91st Annual Forum of the National Conference on Social Welfare, Los Angeles, May, 1964.

We have come away from the two-year project with the encouraging insight that (1) involvement of community resources outside the Court is feasible and institutions not primarily concerned with corrections (e.g., schools) are approachable; (2) the idea of systematic work in Corrections, involving the recognition of complex causes of delinquent behavior and the setting up of complex ways of coping with it, is neither alien nor necessarily frightening to people already working in the field; and (3) until such time when generic social work curricula have been worked out and generically trained workers become available, systematization of Correctional work can be started by well-planned in-service training efforts in which workers in the field have an opportunity to learn from one another.[5]

In the present chapter I will attempt to give a comprehensive statement on the complexity and diversity of social problems, based on some of the materials contained in preceding pages; thoughts on how generic social work may provide the skills needed to take on such complexities and how it has greater potential for systematic work than social work in its conventional organization about specialized methods. Finally, the logic of systematic social work will be demonstrated in its application to corrections.

The reader interested in the reaction which workers in the field may show to such a reorientation are encouraged to turn to Appendix B. It contains excerpts from the week-long discussion in our 1964 institute workshops and a content analysis of these showing the degree of attention given to those areas of thought and action we had hoped to work on, namely some of the particulars involved in the notion that *Corrections is a community effort.*

B. Diversity and Complexity of Social Problems.

1. Deviance and Delinquency.

The concept of deviance implies the existence of norms, com-

[5] Some participants of our institutes told us that this latter aspect was of more use to them than the program of lectures. We would like to think, however, that such lectures as were provided for them helped to focus their attention on the area we wanted to develop: Community involvement.

pliance with which is desirable. These norms vary from place
to place and from society to society. Therefore, deviance cannot
be defined descriptively by referring to a set of specific acts. It
must be defined as a failure to comply with the norms of the
social group within which an individual operates. Inasmuch as it
is largely the middle class norms that have been elevated into
legal standards for our society, *delinquency* is generally definable
as deviance from middle class norms.

2. Social Class and Ethnic Value Discrepancies.

Students of social stratification and of race and ethnic relations are familiar with the variations of world view, traditions,
and perception used by members of different subgroupings in our
society. Values vary among groups. We have referred before to
W. F. Whyte's study of lower class sex mores, indicating that
such mores are different from those of the middle classes (which
latter are reflected in law), but they are not absent. Similarly,
attitudes toward education, ambition, job performance, etc., of
lower class people are different from the ones espoused by middle
class, pace-setting America. There was a time when Indians
were thought to be demonstrably less intelligent than whites,
because their children would consistently score low on intelli-
gence tests. Eventually it was found that their low I.Q. was due
to their noncompetitive attitude in the area of verbal expression.
Instructions to "work as fast as you can" do not evoke in them
their highest possible performance. Speed and time are familiar
and important concepts to most people in Western culture, but
not necessarily to others. We must therefore take cultural backgrounds into consideration before we can make fair comparisons
between people.

We are again reminded of G. H. Mead's definition of value
as an object in its capacity to satisfy an interest. This points to
a convergence of the concept of *value-system* with that of *motivation*. People with like value systems can be expected to be similarly motivated, provided their situations (or "fields," or "life space"
in Kurt Lewin's terms) are also similar. People with different or
dissimilar value systems, however, may be very differently moti-

vated, and may act very differently, even under seemingly identical circumstances. Furthermore, not only the aggregate of individual motives, but modes of thought and reasoning vary with the culture in which a person is involved, so that in contacts between people from different cultural (or "subcultural," or "social") backgrounds, e.g., between a middle class social worker and a lower class client, there may be disagreement on objectives and values as well as misunderstanding and overt or covert lack of communication. Ambition, striving for success, concern with one's career, for example, is typical upper-middle class behavior. Working class people, who are typically satisfied to "get by," seeking mainly a safe base for the necessities of life, may not respond very well to rational arguments concerning ways to "better themselves" or "to get ahead." Much less this would be the case with lower class people, who constitute so great a proportion of the social work clientele. Lower class life is found to be pervaded by apathy, a sense of helplessness, of the good life being a matter of luck.[6]

3. Complexity of Motives.

We know that there are variations not only by socio-cultural background, but also in time and by the situation in which an individual finds himself. The many motives behind our behavior are interrelated, changing in strength, and some, at a given time, are stronger than others and therefore dominant. As the pattern of relative deprivation changes, so does the pattern of motives, which explains why we do not have the same thing on our minds all the time.[7] Moreover, *individual and cultural variations interact, for which reason all the behavioral sciences may be necessary to understand crime and delinquency* (and "acceptable" behavior, too, for that matter).

For further clarification of that point, let us explore some of the contingencies of behavior.

---

[6] This descriptive reference to class differences is borrowed from Joseph A. Kahl, *The American Class Structure,* New York, Rinehart, 1957, *passim.*

[7] Cf. Abram Maslow, *Motivation and Personality,* New York, Harper, 1954, *passim.*

4. Interaction of Social and Individual Variables.

Cloward and Ohlin distinguish three types of delinquency, *criminal, conflict,* and *retreatist,* each of which is likely to appear in a different combination of circumstances.[8] The degree to which "official" social norms have been internalized, and the relative access to one's goals by legitimate or illegitimate means, are of consequence. The different possibilities and their probable outcomes are given in tabular form (for clarity, relative internalization of norms—psychoanalysts would say development of a superego—has been dichotomized):

	Norms not, or inadequately internalized	*Norms well internalized*
Legitimate channels open	"Middle Class delinquency" and delinquency due to psychological factors	Low incidence of delinquency
Legitimate channels closed. Illegitimate channels open	Rational, criminal type of delinquency ("crime for profit," career criminality)	
All channels closed	Irrational delinquency (violence, vandalism)	Withdrawal (e.g., drug addiction)

As the internalization of norms and access to goals by legitimate and illegitimate means vary, we may expect that in the majority of cases we get mixed types of delinquency. Besides, there are contingencies not mentioned so far, though implied. For example, one condition for the accessibility of success goals through illegitimate means is the presence of an illegitimate structure of criminal activities. Stealing for profit, for instance, is feasible in the long run only if there are fences. Also, "relative internalization of norms" may have to be modified by some

---

[8] Richard A. Cloward and Lloyd E. Ohlin, *New Perspectives on Juvenile Delinquency* (New York School of Social Work, Columbia University, 1959), *passim.*

reference to the interpersonal skills of the individual. Presumably, the retreatist solution is typically used by persons suffering from alienation, defective interpersonal contact with others.[9] Besides, there is the possibility of effective social norms being absent or rare in a society or a segment thereof, in which case we speak of *anomie*. Following the above schema, the hypothesis suggests itself that all other things being equal the incidence of the violent type delinquency varies with anomie.

This is not a systematic review of all the relevant variables that might enter into the understanding of delinquency. The intention is to give an impression of the diverse and complex ways in which delinquency comes about: It stands to reason that remedial action would have to be based on a consideration of these, and that diverse and complex skills on the side of those who take on the problem are necessary. Thus, a youngster whose main problem is a defect in his relationship with his parents and shows delinquent behavior as a consequence may be a good prospect for casework. If, however, his problem consists of defective socialization of a kind typical in this environment, i.e., if he comes from what we see as a delinquent subculture, casework may be effective only if he can be isolated from that subculture, and we then have to ask whether successful work with him does not ignore the larger problem, *namely the integration of the social group from which he comes (with respect to values) into the larger society*. That very clearly exceeds the capacities of the caseworker or the clinical psychologist. The community organizer, aiming at that condition, would have to find or establish not only agencies interested in doing more casework inside the area concerned, but may have to mobilize whatever forces he could find to create community responsibility. Such a task is staggeringly complex, especially when it runs counter to some of the special interests of the larger society. For example, con-

[9] Isador Chein, *Studies on Narcotic Use Among Juveniles*, Research Center for Human Relations, New York University, 1956 (mimeographed). Quoted by Mortimer Fleishhacker, Jr., Committee on Youth, Social Planning Committee, United Community Fund of San Francisco, *Juvenile Delinquency, An Analysis of Theory and Research Toward a Program of Action*, United Community Fund of San Francisco, 1961, pp. 108-109. This analysis contains an excellent overview of existing knowledge and thought in the field, especially pp. 42-57 and pp. 104-261.

ventional slum clearance projects have been concerned with physical improvement, but ignored the fact that the human groups comprising slum communities were torn apart. Similarly, neighborhoods may deteriorate because of highway construction or other face-lifting activities that displace people and encourage the accumulation of transients.

What seems to be needed to improve on the present state of the art in corrections are:

a. *Typologies* of social problems involving unacceptable behavior, and of appropriate treatment procedures.

b. *Public redefinition* of offenders as correctible and worthy; this is an educational effort which would retain the worth of the individual by limiting his delinquent behavior without allowing him to be victimized by an erroneous or unjustified notion of personal responsibility in a situation where people respond to destructive forces over which they have little or no control.

c. *A workable legal framework* for juvenile corrections, combining the treatment aspect of the principle of *parens patriae* and the protection afforded defendants in criminal procedures.

d. *Design of a model* of correctional work that makes possible the use of appropriate treatment methods or social action according to the problems at hand.

C. Toward Generic Social Work.

While help given to existing services by correctional workers may facilitate community action, in itself this is insufficient for an integrated attack on juvenile delinquency, because community resources are poorly coordinated.[10] Personal cooperation on the case level, even systematic case coordination (staffings) is inadequate. Program coordination is necessary, featuring (a) coordination of agency programs, not centered on individual cases,

---

10 National Institute of Mental Health and Children's Bureau, etc., *Report to the Congress on Juvenile Delinquency* (Washington, D. C.: Government Printing Office, 1957), p. 9. Quoted by W. Reid, *op. cit.*, p. 418.

but on the typical problems encountered in the field; (b) the best possible rational alignment of agency functions with existing needs; (c) commitment of considerable resources to coordination.

1. Inadequacy of Conventional Thought.

As was observed at the Arden House Conference of June, 1964, there is much confusion concerning the question of which tasks require social work training and which require a different kind of preparation. This confusion may be based on a kind of reverse logic applied to the problem as formulated there. Professional training should be geared to the needs in the field. It makes little sense to take the available training for granted and argue about which tasks fit the training, although this kind of thinking must be behind the "insular self-sufficiency" of some welfare agencies mentioned by Reid.[11]

Training should be adjusted to the tasks at hand. Inasmuch as the growing recognition of the complexity of social welfare problems makes early specialization a tactic of doubtful value, the skills offered the student should be such that he can enter not only a variety of settings, but develop further in a variety, or use a combination, of methods. The knowledge and the skills needed are to be specified, not the disciplines that provide them.

2. Generic Content and Multilateral Thinking.

The Arden House Conference also suggested that students of correctional skills be exposed to knowledge from a variety of helping disciplines: psychology, education, nursing, medicine, law, vocational counseling, etc.; furthermore, there should be field experience involved in this exposure, *provided formal seminars and conferences with members of these disciplines can be arranged*. This is obviously based on the notion that there must be exposure and follow-up in which a student has an opportunity to digest what he has seen, so that he learns to put himself in the position of the other worker and, in time, learns to see problems in perspective—both with respect to their genesis

---

[11] Reid, *op. cit.*, p. 424.

and in terms of appropriate remedial action. While nobody can be expected to be thoroughly competent in all these fields, enough knowledge about the complexity of the problems and their treatment ought to be acquired to enable a worker to judge whether his own skills are appropriate and sufficient to handle a case.

Some people in the field might argue that this problem is recognized and being handled. Referrals *are* made; diagnostic facilities, both medical and psychological, *are* employed; casework *does* go beyond contact with the individual. However, we know that often what is taught in school cannot be practiced, e.g., in correctional work, where large caseloads make intensive supervision difficult and involvement of the family, of schools, churches, etc., next to impossible. We are faced with a vicious circle: As the pressures of a large caseload keep a worker's involvement with a client at the bare minimum (and perhaps below the minimum necessary for success), stable working relationships with other agencies, let alone institutions not primarily concerned with welfare work, cannot develop. At the same time it seems that once the circle is broken, the resulting systematic approach might have two effects: (a) lower incidence of delinquency, because problems are attacked at their roots; (b) more time per worker that can be used for proper casework.

3. Implications for Training and Practice.

A frequent criticism of the idea of generic social work training is that it would produce workers who "can't do anything well." This apprehension is partly justified, though for the wrong reasons. The critics commonly assume that the generic social worker would, in his two years of professional training, receive but a smattering of casework, group work, and community organization experience and would have to be trained on the job. This latter requirement, it seems, exists to some degree even with respect to conventionally trained social workers, although to different degrees in different methods. It would be accentuated in the case of generically trained people, *not because of the inadequacy of training, but because of the present organization of the welfare professions.* Putting it bluntly: At the present time, many welfare agencies might not know what to do with a worker who cannot say that he is specialized in at least one of the social work methods.

Let us illustrate the situation by referring to the medical profession, where we can find a fitting analogy:

Preparation for medical training proper consists of work in physical and life sciences. Later on, knowledge in a variety of specialized disciplines is acquired, all mutually related, but not even as an aggregate constituting the essence of medical know-how. It is not the "sum total" of anatomy, physiology, bacteriology, pathology, internal medicine and surgery that makes a person a competent physician, but the *integration* of all of these into diagnosis and a treatment plan as he is confronted with a case. While the skill of applying one's knowledge of the basics and of symptomatology is part of clinical training, it is probably the period of *internship* that really makes a doctor.

Similarly, all the knowledge and incipient skills a social work student is able to acquire in the two years of professional training will not make him a competent social worker, and that would probably be more true of a generically trained person than of one whose field training has been specialized from the beginning. For while specialization at an early stage will tend to black out much learning in the methods not chosen for intensive instruction, the limited scope of training in existing methods brings competence in such a method within reach. Generic social work, on the other hand, avoids the "blinders" of early specialization, but since it is a way to take on tremendously complex problems, the time necessary for the development of a professional capacity to function in this new mode of social work must be expected to be more than is now available during the two years of training.

We are suggesting that specialization take place not during the two years of attending a school of social work, but, if at all, during the first one or two years of professionally supervised practice. (This in further analogy to the medical model: Training of a physician involves internship and residency and does not end with the acquisition of a degree.) An additional benefit of later specialization in social work training is the greater opportunity of students to choose a field of practice and concentrate on those methods which make the best possible use of their talents.

The existing structure of the social work profession already provides a framework for that. Needed is only a redefinition of the fully trained social worker as someone who is eligible for membership in the Academy of Certified Social Workers, perhaps with some additional specifications concerning the nature of placement and supervision during his "internship." The lengthening of the process of training is justified by the often decisive influence social workers are expected to have on the lives of others. Let us return once more to the medical model.

Even with complete medical training, there are problems no physician will take on alone. One kind is the "special case," which he will either refer to a specialist or on which he will bring in a colleague. A second kind of problem, more interesting to us, is *epidemics*. No competent doctor would discover a half dozen cases of cholera or dysentery and be content to treat individual cases as they came to his attention. Nor would the community expect him to. Since the etiology of these diseases is known, large-scale, organized, communal action would be taken: Wells would be checked for contamination, patients isolated, perhaps schools closed; people would be advised against the drinking of unboiled water, perhaps a quarantine would be established. The whole effort of fighting an epidemic is one involving many skills, many roles, many institutions. No one claims primary leadership, and no one, including the physicians, would hold that the treatment of individual victims were the core of the effort (although the patients have every right to feel that way).

To us, two features of the medical model are of interest: First, the competence of the individual practitioner depends on the integration of diverse kinds of knowledge, some of them but indirectly related to everyday practice. Secondly, even the accomplished professional will encounter problems with which he cannot possibly, and is not expected to, cope alone.

It might be argued that epidemiology is only partly medicine, and partly a social concern with public health. True social epidemiology (I do wish the term were common) can, analogously, be seen as only partly social work, and partly public concern with social welfare: The analogy fits.

The weakness of the epidemiological approach to welfare problems is twofold: First, the supporting disciplines of social work are not nearly as developed as those of medicine. The behavioral sciences are younger, less differentiated and less positive with respect to their results than physical and life sciences; secondly, the public is well aware of the need for hygiene, balanced diets and the kind of contingencies that determine physical health, and doctors are held in high esteem. Next to nothing like this can be said about public knowledge or attitudes toward social problems, although there is hope that this may change in the future.

These weaknesses explain why social workers in general and correctional workers in particular do not operate like physicians. They do not explain why *available* knowledge is so inadequately used.

4. Redefinition of "Client."

One other difficulty with the application of the medical model to social work is the uncertainty concerning the history behind an individual case. How one contracts the flu, tuberculosis or cholera is fairly well known, and an epidemic can be defined in terms of incidence. It is not as easy in the social sphere. The same kinds of symptoms—behavioral symptoms—may be found in different people for very different reasons. From the standpoint of a social therapist, the genesis of inadequate or unacceptable behavior is more important to know than its existence. Motives (including inhibitions) may have physical or intra-psychic origins, may be rooted in interpersonal relationships or, as we have discussed at length, may be based on shared norms of a subculture. Depending on the constellation of individual, group, or socially based motivations, the choice of therapy will have to vary. Inasmuch as the motivational background of visible behavior may not immediately be known, two decisions have to be withheld: What kind of client we are dealing with (is it an individual, a family, a peer group, a delinquent subculture) and what mode of attack on the problem is most promising (is it psychiatric casework, insight therapy, marital counselling of parents, group work with a street gang, or a program for neighborhood rehabilitation)?

This will perhaps become clearer if we start from the fact that social work is a problem solving process. A "case" is actually a problem, not a person. The very name of the profession implies that the problems tackled by it are social, not individual, and that the work must therefore involve more than one person. Preoccupation with individual reactions to social problems has been traditional among caseworkers, which is reflected in the language they use. Social work comprises more than casework, however. If we realize that social problems cover a wide range of complexity and are part of the social system within which we operate, we will also understand why, increasingly, social work theory speaks of the *client system,* which term really describes a problem system, with people as "carriers." Who these people are, how many they are, and in which way they are related to one another will become apparent only in the course of treatment. In our view, this is one of the main arguments for the development of generic social work.

A frequent criticism of existing practices in probation (and the treatment of the mentally ill, incidentally) is that all therapeutic efforts may be for naught if a person is returned to, or remains in, the same environment that helped him develop his problems in the first place. The counter argument runs something like this: Successful therapy, or supervision, will leave an individual changed, strengthened, more resilient, insightful, responsible, etc., so therefore his own environment is no longer the same for him. This view can, of course, be supported from the point of view of the social psychology as developed in Chapter III. The question remains, however, whether we want to be content with the prospect of increasing the resistance of individuals to social forces known to be stressful, potentially destructive and opposed to the full development of the positive side of people's potential. Contemporary social work, and especially corrections, is essentially defensive.

This critique seems to imply that preventive action ought to accompany, or supplement, efforts at the treatment of offenders. As we see it, however, *the concept of the client system and generic social work as the attendant mode of working with that system obliterate the distinction between treatment and prevention.* We know that delinquency rates are not due to the aggregates of individual behaviors. Inasmuch as our ideology and concepts of justice hold individuals responsible for individual acts, we will have to continue to pay attention to the motives and the situation of individuals. Casework is not obsolescent.

But we know that social conditions quite beyond the grasp and certainly beyond the control of individual offenders exist whose modification would do much to alleviate the problem. Such modification should be a *systematic* undertaking for which conventional training in social work or any other of the helping professions, as presently organized, does not equip the practitioner.

D. Conclusion: Corrections as Community Resocialization.

The resocialization approach takes the environment *as a system* into account. By a system is meant, in this context, an arrangement of individuals, groups, and institutions that are related to one another in a complex of interaction. The helping process in corrections aims at the system as well as the individual offender. What specific acts are necessary to effect significant change continues to depend on the case. Whether the techniques used will come through what is now known as the methods of casework, group work or community organization, or what combination of these will be employed, will become clear only as the *client system* is understood and appropriate action taken. Decisions on method *cannot be made in advance.*

The development of a correctional system capable of achieving complex tasks (e.g., by developing a correctional force of generically trained workers attacking the delinquent client system) is mandatory for the following reasons:

(1) Personality is in part an expression of culture. Many individual acts, including "unacceptable" behavior, are grounded in mores and folkways, in cultures whose values are at variance with the official norms of our society. Therefore, the correctional system must be capable of (a) discovering what delinquent behavior is culturally grounded and (b) attack a "case" on individual, group, and community (cultural) levels at the same time.

(2) Our society is complex, consisting not only of different classes whose value systems vary, but also of groups which differ with respect to their position on the "folk-urban" scale: Some groups are small, cohesive, with close ties between people and human relationships are face-to-face. Others are large, with tenuous and segmental relationships between people who know one another only in a limited number of roles, and where no one is anybody else's keeper. Contact between groups so divergent creates problems typical of a modern, complex, industrial society. The correctional system must be able to recognize, in diagnosis as well as treatment, that not only is individual behavior in part socially determined, but the social milieu itself varies with the composition of a community (e.g., certain ethnic groups may be peaceful and content when living by themselves, but turn to violence when they have to share a neighborhood with certain other ethnic groups).

(3) Some sections of our society may be anomic. That means that commonly accepted norms are rare or absent. One could describe these as morally amorphous. In these cases, one could say that the aggregate population in such groups does not actually form a community. Neither casework nor group work alone could therefore succeed in correcting social ills. A community may have to be created by mobilizing whatever resources, institutional or otherwise, are available, *plus* follow-through on the case or group level.

(4) To compound our problem, we may find that in the more amorphous parts of society there is little or no rational socialization of the young, or the channels of socialization are unknown. This not only makes the social diagnosis difficult (e.g., finding

out which "others" in a particular youngster's life are significant and therefore important to the treatment process), but might give correctional workers the impression that every case is one of a kind. Only a Correctional *system* capable of handling the problem of juvenile delinquency will succeed in discovering regularities and "hidden" social causes and in bringing to bear all of the talent and skills of the people working in it.

To take on the problem of crime and delinquency in such a complex environment, it seems any of three approaches, or a combination of them, must be used: First, *coordination* of existing services, secondly, *integration* into the training of correctional personnel of knowledge from a variety of supporting disciplines and broadening the base of professional skill prior to specialization, and thirdly, *systematization* of correctional work.

The first of these, coordination, is the job of community organization people, quite possible on the basis of existing know-how, but rare, difficult and expensive.

The second approach is largely contained in the suggested shift toward generic social work as discussed above; it is involved, time consuming and costly as compared to present training procedures, but possibly a good investment of time, talent and money with respect to the return from workers on the job.

The third approach should really be viewed as a corollary of the second. It constitutes a reorganization (revision) of present correctional practice, for which generic training would prepare the social worker. A diagram might help to clarify the relationship between these three approaches:

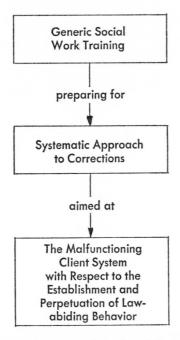

Figure 2: Generic Social Work and Corrections.

A great number of problems that would make the realization of such a scheme difficult have not even been touched upon. How, for example, are the various efforts at community re-socialization, i.e., the therapy centering on a whole set of defective relationships, to be effected, when a Correctional officer, under existing law, "has" authority only over one individual? How are certain welfare agencies to be persuaded to relinquish their "insular self-sufficiency," in the interest of coordination or systematization? How can schools of social work modify their program toward generic social work and adequately prepare students for professional practice, while existing welfare agencies, including probation departments, have a "wait-and-see" attitude and are organized around conventional methods? How is the public to be won over to the idea that corrections is a community effort and increased expenditures for social therapy are a good investment in the long run?

We have no answers to these questions, but that was not the

purpose of this essay. It was to provide a new perspective. It is our hope that others may be stimulated by some of these ideas and use them in their work.

APPENDIX

APPENDIX A

Introduction to the 1964 Institute for Juvenile
Correctional Officers and Related Personnel
At Saint Louis University
Roster of Institute Personnel
and Brief Institute Outline

A SECOND JUVENILE OFFICERS CORRECTIONAL TRAINING INSTITUTE

June 14-19, 1964

An Institute for Missouri
Juvenile Correctional Officers

Sponsored By

SAINT LOUIS UNIVERSITY

SCHOOL OF SOCIAL SERVICE

INSTITUTE FOR DELINQUENCY CONTROL

and

THE SAINT LOUIS CITY JUVENILE COURT

Made possible under a Grant from the President's Committee

on Juvenile Delinquency and Youth Development

Introduction

The 1964 Institute for Juvenile Correctional Personnel is part of a continuing effort at providing in-service training for people already in the field of corrections. While the first Institute in the summer of 1963 was primarily concerned with knowledge and skills utilized in individual treatment, this year's Institute will address itself to *the problems of mobilization of resources outside the Court and the interaction of the Court with the community*.

The rationale of this is expressed in the theme "Corrections Is a Community Effort." This implies the notion that the effectiveness of probation is increased if the Court's efforts can be complemented by the wise use of those institutions (family, school, etc.) with which youngsters have frequent and sustained contact.

It also implies that the correctional process is not and never was an isolated function. The roots of the problem lie in the community and our society, and, while unseemingly difficult of definition and solution, are no more separable from the community, than is the community's responsibility for the adequate functioning of its Courts and implementation of its laws.

The Court function is only one phase of the juvenile correctional process. The police, institutional, parole and placement personnel, as well as others, have their respective responsibilities to the community. How well the whole process works, considering overlapping authority, interest and purpose, is heavily dependent on knowledge, the personalities involved, and above all the understanding, interest and determination of the community to accept responsibility for its efficient functioning.

In this sense the correctional field is directly involved in the political life of the community. Keeping this basic fact in mind should instill in the correctional worker and his Court the urgent necessity to place a continued emphasis on an on-going interpretation of "why we are doing what we are doing," regardless of immediate superficial reactions.

Problems become more readily solvable when adequate facts are available and understood. The field of corrections can ill afford the growing tendency to ascribe responsibility to any given agency or institution for juvenile deliquency and crime. Allowing myths and misunderstood facts about corrections to build up and accumulate in any given community does not foster good correctional resources.

To allow the Juvenile Court idea to be tested, it must first be tried. To date very few jurisdictions have made this possible. Many voices from the community are heard that the idea has failed and that we ought to look for something different, while in the same breath withholding the necessary resources and interest to do the job.

It is the wish and intention of the Institute planners to add even in a slight way to the accumulated knowledge and interest of those attending to the end of ever seeking advancement of correctional skills and techniques.

We hope you find the materials of interest and value.

> Bernard J. Coughlin, S.J.
> Project Director
>
> J. E. Garrett,
> Associate Director
>
> Peter O. Rompler,
> Project Research Analyst

INSTITUTE OBJECTIVES

A. To thoroughly explore the position of the Juvenile Court in the community and to understand that "Corrections" is not an isolated process.

B. To identify ways to help the community better understand the problems of juvenile correction.

C. To help promote better community-court relationships by improvement in the areas of:

    1. Coordination of community services.

    2. Communication among agencies.

    3. Utilization of community resources.

ADMINISTRATION, FACULTY, CONSULTANTS AND SPEAKERS

ADMINISTRATION

Very Reverend Paul C. Reinert, S.J., President, St. Louis University

Reverend Bernard J. Coughlin, S.J., Director, School of Social Service, Director, Institute of Delinquency Control

James E. Garrett, Training Demonstration Project Coordinator, Institute of Deliquency Control, School of Social Service, St. Louis University

Peter O. Rompler, Director of Project Research and Evaluation

FACULTY AND CONSULTANTS

Mr. Bernard Kogon, Director of Training, Los Angeles County Probation Department, Institute Faculty Chairman

Dr. Gilbert Geis, Professor of Sociology and Criminology, Los Angeles State College

Professor Charles Newman, Director of Correctional Training, Kent School of Social Work, University of Louisville

Judge Michael Carroll, Juvenile Judge, Circuit Court of St. Louis County

Dr. Warren Brown, Assistant Superintendent, Ferguson-Florissant Reorganized School District

Riley Eddleman, Director of Guidance, Hazelwood School District

Dr. George Ulett, Director, Division of Mental Diseases, State of Missouri

Lorena Scherer, Supervisor, State Child Welfare Services, Division of Welfare, State of Missouri

R. W. Kottkamp, Supervisor of Vocational Training, O'Fallon High School, City of St. Louis

Sgt. Amon Owens, Webster Groves Police Department, President, St. Louis Juvenile Officers Assoc.

VISITING PANEL PARTICIPANTS

Eugene Schwartz, Executive Director, Metropolitan Youth Commission of St. Louis

Perrian Winget, Juvenile Officer, Mexico, Missouri, Training-Demonstration Project Workshop Coordinator in Kansas City, Missouri

Forrest Swall, Community Development Agent, Washington County, University of Missouri Extension Center

INSTITUTE DISCUSSION LEADERS

Miss Mary K. Mullins, Chief Deputy Juvenile Officer, St. Louis City Juvenile Court; Field Instructor, St. Louis University School of Social Service

Joseph Gorman, Supervisor, St. Louis County Juvenile Court

William Hennessy, Director, St. Louis County Adult Probation Department

Miss Dorothy F. Roberts, Juvenile Officer, Nevada, Missouri

Forrest Swall, Community Development Agent, Washington County, University of Missouri Extension Center, Potosi, Missouri

INSTITUTE TRAINING CONSULTANT

John O'Brien, Administrator, Juvenile Division, Circuit Court, City of St. Louis

INSTITUTE GUEST SPEAKERS

Judge Laurance M. Hyde, Jr., Presiding Judge, Juvenile Division, Circuit Court, City of St. Louis

Donald Blackburn, Director, Jackson County Children's Institutions, Kansas City, Missouri

Milton Epstein, Chairman of the Board, Industrial Engineering and Equipment Company, St. Louis, Missouri; also Chairman, Corrections Committee, Missouri Association for Social Welfare

"CORRECTIONS IS A COMMUNITY EFFORT"

Schedule, June 14-19, 1964

A Second Juvenile Correctional Officers Training Institute

SUNDAY 6-14	MONDAY 6-15	TUESDAY 6-16	WEDNESDAY 6-17	THURSDAY 6-18	FRIDAY 6-19
	What Kind of Animal is the Juvenile Court?	Intake Community Agency Relationships	Available Community Resources: Use and Limitations	Integration of Community Resources	Review and Summary
	9:00-9:50 Judge Carroll: Role and Function of the Court	9:00-9:50 School Admin. and Juv. Ct. Problems	9:00-9:45 Child Welfare —Juvenile Ct. Relationships	9:00-10:20 Prof. Chas. Newman: Overall Correctional Directions	9:00-9:50 Sociological Concepts
	10:00-10:50 Concepts of Role and Institution	10:00-10:50 School Guidance & Juvenile Ct. Problems	9:50-10:30 Mental Health —Juvenile Ct. Relationships	Prof. Chas. Newman	10:00-10:50 Correctional Concepts
	11:00-11:50 Workshop I	11:00-11:50 Workshop I	10:40-11:20 Creation of Employment Opportunities 11:30-12:00 Panel of Resources	10:30-11:50 Panel Reaction and Questions	11:00-11:50 Workshop
	LUNCH	LUNCH	LUNCH	LUNCH	12:00-1:30 Dinner and Closing Speaker
	1:30-2:10 Ben Kogon: Correction Concepts	1:30-2:20 Enforcement Personnel Paper	1:30-2:20 Soc. and Cor. Comment	1:30-2:20 Soc. & Cor. Comment	
Afternoon: Arrival of Participants	2:20-2:50 Causation Factors	2:30-2:50 Ben Kogon: Summary	2:30-4:00 Workshop	2:30-4:00 Workshop	
7:30-10:00 p.m.	3:00-4:00 Workshop II	3:00-4:00 Workshop II			
Registration and Welcome Reception— Fr. Coughlin Judge Hyde	4:10-5:00 Faculty----	4:10-5:00	4:10-5:00	4:10-5:00 Conference 7:30-10:00 Reception & Speaker	

APPENDIX B

Content Analysis of Workshop Discussions

Peter O. Rompler

CONTENT ANALYSIS OF WORKSHOP DISCUSSIONS

1. Introduction.

The Institute For Delinquency Control of the Saint Louis University School of Social Service conducted Institutes For Juvenile Correctional Officers and Related Personnel in 1963 and 1964. Both Institutes were one week in duration and provided lectures by specialists in various fields as well as group discussion in which the material could be related to the participants' work experience. The discussion sessions occupied about half of the time schedule.

In both years, the Institute was followed up by a series of seven or eight monthly workshops of about four hours duration. They were held in two different locations and continued the work of the Institute, with increased active participation by trainees and attention being given to problems arising out of practice.

The 1963 Institute had sought to impart some applicable knowledge from the fields of psychiatry, sociology and probation. In 1964, it was the need for the involvement of resources outside the court on which we focused attention, the theme of the Institute being: "Corrections is a Community Effort." The theoretical basis for this orientation as well as some facets of planned action that would lead to modification of present practice have been developed in the preceding four chapters.

While the 1964 Institute was being planned, we did not know whether the participants, representing different agencies and various kinds and degrees of preparation, would be willing to look far beyond the demands of their immediate jobs and be open to the suggestion that one's own effectiveness might be increased through understanding of the capacities and limitations of persons working in other agencies and by involving them in a planned fashion in the job of corrections which was no longer to be viewed as primarily a one-to-one relationship between worker and individual client.

(a) *Purpose.* Since the aims of our Project included demonstration of the effectiveness of the training method, we had to find ways of showing that the Institute objectives were met. One indication of success is the taking up of the day's material in discussion groups and the degree to which the discussions follow the theme of the training effort. The latter aspect was of special interest to us, since we expected the participants to have difficulty with the handling of complex problems, even if they were couched in practical terms. To find out what topics came up in the group sessions, how often they came up and at what time during the week of the Institute, was the purpose of this content analysis.

(b) *Method*. Each day during the Institutes, a number of discussion sessions was tape recorded. In 1963, the recordings were arranged so as to include each of the five groups at one time or another. In 1964, we were primarily interested in showing the development of the discussions during the week and therefore obtained recordings from the same group every day plus recordings from several other groups.

From the tape recordings, a roster of exchanges between the participants was compiled. Next, those responses that seemed to relate to one another were grouped together and each of these groups was given a heading that would describe the underlying theme. The themes were ordered by the frequency with which responses relating to them occurred in the 1964 Institute. All responses recorded and the themes under which they were subsumed are given in Section 4, Tables la through li (for the 1963 Institute) and in Tables 2a through 2h (for 1964). It will be noticed that the same responses are often relevant with respect to more than one theme and were so recorded. For example, *mobilization of resources* (Table 2d) was discussed in such a way that it seemed relevant under "professionalism" as well as "systems thought" and "social structure and function."

The meaning of the thematic headings should be clear from the responses listed under them. I will only mention that by "systems thought" was meant any reference to complex causation of delinquency, or to socio-cultural contingencies in interaction and the need for coordination of resources, alignment of treatment facilities with needs, and problems of feedback.

To describe the relative attention given to the various themes throughout the Institutes, a measure of "proportional incidence" was introduced. It is defined as

$$P.I. = 100 \frac{N}{n},$$

where N is the number of times a response or exchange was relevant to the theme in question and n is the total number of exchanges counted during a particular workshop session. The proportional incidence of the six themes is listed, workshop by workshop, in Tables 3 (for 1963) and 4 (for 1964).[1]

Tables 5, 6, and 7 offer comparisons between the 1963 and 1964 Institutes. Graph I is largely a display of data from Table 7. The significance of these comparisons will be discussed later.

---

[1] Since, as was explained above, one response was often relevant to more than one theme, the proportional incidence index is not a percentage. The values for P.I. within one workshop usually add up to more than 100.

2. The Material: Annotated Excerpts From Discussion Sessions.

The following is a collection of quotes from the Institute Workshops and one Follow-up Workshop. The progress of the discussions illustrates the increasing concern on the side of the participants with the implications of the theme of the 1964 Institute ("Corrections is a Community Effort"). All quotes from the Summer Institute Workshop came from Group III.[2] Discussion leaders were rotated. There were daily discussion sessions in the Institute, usually one in the morning (50 minutes) and one in the afternoon (1½ hours). Discussion leaders and time of the recording are given at the beginning of each session reported here.

Group III consisted of three case workers (B, E[3], X), one group worker (A), one police officer (C), one placement officer of the State Board of Training Schools (D), and one juvenile officer with a law degree (F). "DL" identifies the discussion leader[4] whose name is given in the heading of each session.

Parentheses contain either summaries of participants' responses or passages supplied by the analyst when the recording was unclear. Editorial comments are in brackets.

[Mary] *Kate Mullins, Monday, a.m.*

In this early session the members of the group are still getting acquainted and are not yet attuned to the objectives of the discussion groups. It is evident that questions by the discussion leader are taken more concretely than they may have been intended. For example, after the members of the group have introduced themselves they go into a discussion of the materials presented that morning. C reacts to the presentation by Gilbert Geis.[5] It seems he liked his ideas, especially those concerning the change of roles in American families.

DL: What effect does that have on juvenile delinquency?

C: Children are learning from us. The image children have of adults has an influence on our problems. Types of juvenile delinquency and types of crime change in time.

DL: What will the community think of things like shelter care and foster homes?

(Answer): Foster care should be cheaper and more therapeutic.

DL: Does social change imply a change in services? Does the juvenile court participate in community change?

---

[2] i.e., one group out of five.
[3] Not represented in the transcript.
[4] For the background of the workshop discussion leaders, see Appendix A, page 90.
[5] Gilbert Geis, Ph.D., Professor of Sociology and Criminology, Los Angeles State College.

(Answer): The court has a role to play, but placement in foster homes is the responsibility of child welfare services.

The group is still concerned with the immediate and misses the abstraction intended by the discussion leader's questions. At this point, one of the participants then evidently attempts really to get the discussion off the ground:

A: Do you think we should have a juvenile court?

C: Indeed I do.

A: What should be its purpose?

C: To try people—just as any other court would do. A court is a court. There should be no difference between a juvenile court and other courts.

DL: (Summarizing): The judge or the umpire then are to decide if the court has jurisdiction.

C: The court must also convict. Social workers should come in afterwards . . . in many cases there is extensive workup before a judge ever sees the kid. (Then he talks about a boy, age 16, with a record of 300 burglaries who should have been treated four years ago.)

X: That's rare.

C: It's not rare. It's not a damn bit worse than five.

The discussion leader now asks what the group thinks the reaction of the community is to juvenile court procedures and how they handle it. She also asks them whether the administrators of their respective courts protect them. What do administrators do? The group, however, does not answer her questions but reverts to talking about specific cases. One participant observes that the group agrees on the ultimate purpose but disagrees on the means of achieving it. C objects to children being continued on probation after they violate it. X observes that probation is a form of treatment to which C replies that he agrees that treatment is necessary, but that an incorrigible thief needs residential treatment and not probation. Rather than letting the discussion get lost in specifics, the discussion leader, trying to summarize, observes that (1) the juvenile court has to establish jurisdiction; (2) offenders need treatment, although there is disagreement on the kind of treatment to be offered.

DL: If you recommend a certain disposition and the community disagrees, what kind of response do you make to community pressure?

B: I wouldn't heed to the community.

DL: What about your mandate of and responsibility to society? How do you get the mandate and how do you meet responsibility?

C: I have a list of resources, e.g., pastors, Optimist Clubs whom I can ask for help.

In this first meeting of Group III a relatively small number of people get to talk and the group as a whole refrains from getting into a discussion of the theme of the Institute. The primary concern is with specific cases and specific problems and the questions by the discussion leader are treated accordingly.

Dorothy Roberts, Tuesday a.m.

First evidence that this group is getting interested in the role of community in the treatment of juvenile delinquency comes out of this session. A raises the problem of the degree to which information which juvenile officers have should be shared with others. For example, do you tell school people about an incest case? X observes that teachers are not "as open-minded as we are."

D: School people are hide-bound by yard after yard of their own regulations. They over-emphasize their breach. They also rely on outside help too much, on policemen, the courts, and the Booneville[6] people. Considering the high standards by which teachers are trained and hired, it's pathetic what order of difficulty upsets them.

Counselling begins at second or third grade. They have their test data . . . what do they do with it? [There ensues an animatedly confused discussion on records, their use and exchange. Finally D comes back to his observations on the use of resources.] Why don't schools establish a residence hall for children who need a clean, healthy environment? Let the professionals take over, see how it works.

A: I don't think that is the school's function.

But D seems to think that anything is or should be the school's function that serves to educate.

DL: Does this get into the area of "social services" which Dr. Brown maintains are not a function of the school?

D: He's got it, though, as he proudly announced: social service, food service, health service—fine idea! [D sounds complimentary]

While the group is not yet discussing the role of the community in delinquency treatment and prevention *per se*, there is evidence that the roles and functions of different institutions in the community are seen as overlapping or complementary.

Dorothy Roberts, Tuesday p.m.

The discussion leader starts this meeting by raising the question of the

[6] Reference to the state's training school for boys.

sources of authority. She also wonders how relationships with potential resources can be established to make outside help available to the juvenile officer. The group, however, continues the discussion of the morning:

D: If the school people want information, let them have it. They oversee our subjects eight hours a day.

F: Some superintendents can handle information in a comprehensive manner. Others will jump the kid, harass them. You have to be careful whom you give your information to. Parents may also call you and wonder why you gave it to the school.

A: I always discuss with them my plans, who referred the child and why he is there. (I don't give them) any specifics. The information I want is not confidential (e.g., adjustment to class, school record, attendance record) . . . I never had a situation where the child couldn't tell me as much as the teachers could.

B: I get the impression from you all that the school is informed on their children.

A: (Talks about her relationship with the probationers.)

F: What is your case load?

A: 20.

F: Mine is about 150 (then adds a comment on this making a difference).

C now begins to talk about the work of the police and A asks him about what happens when a child runs away from home: Who picks him up and who questions him? She continues to talk about her own experience with the police and so does F. C then reports that in his community the police have 13 officers in the juvenile department and handle 5000 cases annually. He adds:

Someone got the idea that the police aren't educated enough to do the job. But actually the police department spends more money to train their people than the court does.

The discussion of the group in this session introduced no new knowledge about existing resources but seemed to constitute a critical evaluation of the possibilities of cooperation, the problem of communication between them and the contribution that each could make to delinquency treatment or prevention. Included in this discussion were the capabilities of the agencies or departments represented by the participants in this discussion, and the discussion was searching enough to put some of the participants slightly on the defensive.

Forrest Swall, Wednesday p.m.

The following session, from which we are going to quote more extensively, shows increasing independence from the guidance by the discussion leader and an organically growing interest in the kind of community orientation we were hoping to get across.

The discussion starts out with complaints by C about the lack of reciprocity on the side of agencies other than the police. These agencies will not let him have their records, but expect information from him. He is also annoyed by the fact that other agencies frequently want time during which to arrange for help needed by children. He argues that children in trouble need help immediately.

At this point, D gives the discussion a new turn, supported by the discussion leader and A:

> D: I think I can explain it in a relatively simple fashion. It is probable that there could be dual activity in one person, dual supervision of a case, and in some cases they are miles apart. The police have as its mission the apprehension of criminals. . . .

> C: You forget the most basic task of the police: the prevention of crime.

> X: Let him finish.

> D: All right. You might be geared, your interest might be geared, by the mission of your agency. The mission is different for example between the Division of Welfare and the police, so that agency withdraws within its mission, within its bounds—(Everybody) may want cooperation on his terms. You get it 100 times a week.

The discussion leader briefly reviews at this point what he thinks D had been trying to say: that the lecture in the morning had been one-sided —asking cooperation from other agencies while not dealing with the possibilities of the Division of Welfare offering cooperation to others.[7] C says that that was what he thought.

The reader may notice that in this relatively short exchange of views a number of sophisticated concepts have been mentioned or alluded to: the possibility of *ad hoc* case coordination; the difficulties implied in the absence of such; "agency mission," i.e., its purpose and the ways in which this limits the choices of individuals who work within such an agency (this is what sociologists call "institutional constraint"); finally, the absence of program coordination or even systematic case coordination ("service integration") which makes for friction between individuals operating in similar areas but in different agencies. Apparently sensitive to the operating contingencies of complex bureaucratic structures, A continues the discussion and develops the following:

> A: One part of the problem may be the lack of looking at the realistic problems that a public agency has and which make it difficult for it to

---

[7] A lecture by Miss Lorena Scherer, Supervisor, Child Welfare Services, Division of Welfare, State of Missouri, on available services to juvenile courts, their use and problems involved.

do something for us . . . they should be more honest with us. There are a lot of problems involved: lack of budget, lack of staff and training, and lack of foster homes. *If we know some of the limitations they are up against, it won't be frustrating when we don't get the kind of service they say they want to give.*

It is probably not an accident that this suggestion should have been made by a trained group worker. She apparently decided that groups or even bureaucracies have to be understood from within, in compliance with the casework principle that you have to start where the client is. The policeman in the group, however, reacts to another point she has been making and responds:

> C: Don't misunderstand me. I am not frustrated. There are a dozen ways to go. I don't have to go that way. But: these people are *obligated by law* [emphasis added], by their very mandate. (Our lecturer this morning) said to take care of children in need . . . I have their manual in my desk of what they are supposed to do. We have completely cast it aside as of no value.

Even though C may not have realized it at the time, his point was very closely related to A's: He too was referring to a feature of bureaucracies which may force us to understand them from within. It is the discrepancy between what *ought* to be and what *is* with respect to the rules by which work in these structures progresses. This discrepancy is known as that between professed and operand norms.

A little later F makes an observation concerning another feature of work with large institutions: the phenomenon of blocks to communication. Underlings, he complains, take over for the top man at times and let the latter hear only what he wants to hear. Thus he (F) has been frustrated by an intake worker at the state hospital who would tell him "I can't handle this" and keep him from seeing the director. Apparently prompted by the possibility of the discussion being sidetracked, the discussion leader cuts in at this point and relates these comments back to the larger problem.

> DL: That sabotages your relationship. What does the group suggest F could do? . . . Maybe they are establishing some criteria, some procedure that is different from what it was before. (Maybe) you want to carry on with the old system and they are setting up a new system.

A and D take a turn each at describing the following group of problems: personal and institutional action tend to be confused (A: "People take it personally when you are critical of the budget"). Schools tend to confuse private and public infractions of rules; operating procedures in institutions such as state hospitals may differ from place to place to the extent that each hospital has its own procedures, so that a worker who has to cooperate with a variety of them becomes utterly confused and may miss information necessary for his successful functioning. D illustrates this by relating the case of a girl who was placed, without his prior knowledge, in an experimental community placement program. Three weeks later he was asked to look her up without ever having seen a case record. The solution of the case took many people ("everybody but the governor of the state . . ."), but a staffing solved it in one hour and forty minutes. C corroborates his complaints concerning the fragmentation of resources by reporting that a survey in his county showed that all youth serving agencies are "little kingdoms of their own."

Trying to lead back to the main line of the discussion, A suggests that F call the director of the hospital to get together and discuss policy so ". . . you know exactly what to expect." F, however, is adamant in his insistence that he is dealing with a problem involving but an individual:

F: If I could keep this old bag out of it, I would be in good shape. If she stays out of the picture I am in business.

A: *But she can't.*

F. She is the road block, you see.

C: That's why she should be included.

A: Sure!

B: You have it half solved already. You have recognized the problem.

F: (Changing the subject to youth employment opportunities): What can I do to find vocational training for some young people, 17 to 20 years of age, who have no mentality for high school? Some people can do with their hands what they can't do with their heads.

In the last few minutes this discussion had taken the form of A, C, and D instructing F about the logic of systems thought. F's intake worker-nemesis was presented to him as a person who had a very reduced number of choices to her, in other words, was subject to institutional constraint. In effect, these three informed him that his question, what to do about that woman, was beside the point. Instead, he was advised to see her as part of a system, whose operations he needed to understand if he ever expected to work with it successfully. As F tries to change the subject, the discussion leader intervenes:

DL: This is a specific problem. Let's look at it in terms of the community and community resources. How can we approach these things in the community realistically?

[F will not give up easily]: That's my point, how can I approach this problem realistically and do something about these kids?

A and C now take him up with respect to his example, without however discussing his problem in his terms. Instead of giving him specific advice concerning these particular children, C suggests to involve business people, to form a committee on unemployment; A suggests to go beyond that and establish a vocational high school in the region to prevent dropouts in the future:

> A: People must understand that this is a community need which they can do something about.

D seems to think that this latter idea is unrealistic and suggests instead to let the youngsters go to school in the morning and work in the afternoon for low wages, "coolie-wages." A and D are evidently so involved in "system thinking" that the only realistic cure for F's problem are preventive measures rather than therapeutic ones. The discussion leader attempts to remedy this by relating back to C's suggestion about the recruitment of business people; "How do you do this?" C replies that there are service clubs such as the Optimist, Kiwanis Clubs, churches, and the mayor of the city ("who undoubtedly will be in business there") [apparently thinking of a small town].

> C: You form a committee to help you with this problem. You have lunch, you have a couple of drinks, and you let them tell you how they can help you. And by God let me tell you, they will find something for that job.

> DL: What you are saying is, it's a community problem, not the juvenile officer's problem.

> F: It's not really my problem. The youngsters I am thinking about, but I like to get them before the fact, not after the fact.

> C: Here is the thing. You are in this as police and judicial people, by default. The community is not strong enough to take care of this, you have to get into this. So we get into this, and by organizing the community we get the job done. We prevent crime, and that's what we are for.

This last quotation could pass, so to speak, as the Vulgata of modern correctional work in its directness and popular simplicity. C has joined A and D in their concern for the community as an operating system. A discussion ensues on the question whether the probation officer should be the chairman of such a committee. F, perhaps with some irritation, observes:

> F: You get involved in something that is none of your business. You have enough to do if you do your job.

> C: [Very quietly and patiently]: Anything that keeps a kid out of trouble is worth your time.

> F: Last year I talked to 117 different groups . . . because these people wanted to know something about juvenile delinquency and how to stop it.

DL: Talked to people in the community, agencies, to help them come to grips. . . .

F: [Continues to enumerate school boards he has talked to, in an apparent defense against the instruction he is receiving here.] All of them have their problems, and they may or may not take on your problem.

D: Who is going to be in the driver's seat for all the mobilization; who sees to it that certain missions be accomplished? Where should the center of control lie; within the juvenile court, the faceless mob of committees (which all of us love, as Americans, you know)?

A: I should think, with an agency responsible for finding foster placement. But the question goes beyond that.

D: That is exactly right.

A: The question is who takes the initiative . . . individuals should take the initiative.

D: *What* individuals?

A: All individuals.

D: Me? O.K., there is a very famous group called "they." But I don't buy it, believe that "they"—routine. (Then goes on to oppose the vagueness of the discussion of "community resources".)

C: It took me a while to get that committee, but now it is not too much of a problem. It's only about ten business men or civic leaders . . . that's the kind of resource you are talking about that you use when you don't have any others. Right?

D: Right.

The discussion leader who had fallen silent as soon as the discussion was back on the track now cuts in, in order to change, not the subject, but the perspective. Taking a lead from Gilbert Geis' discussion in the morning he asks about the affect of the probation officer.

DL: How does it relate to your own sensitivity, your need? We have a lot of feeling here (concerning the need of the child and community resources). The community in a sense couldn't care less for some of those kids if they didn't come back. And you feel rather strongly about it. What is your experience?

C: The more I work with kids, the more feeling I have for them; and the more I find out that that little rascal got involved not through his fault, but through some adult's fault, the stronger I feel about it . . . I learn more than they do. . . .

Having included the non-rational element in the discussion, the discussion leader makes a final and summarizing comment:

D.L.: You are struggling for the resources your kids need. I wonder if we are not tending to defend our own agencies, our role, tradition, and our own feelings here, and may be avoiding the opportunity of being a little more objective in the effort of reaching out, utilizing existing resources, and developing other resources. But you did a real good job of suggesting ways and means of more involvement of the community. I feel we still came back to the idea that it is *our* problem, *we* have to take care of it. Somehow I kept feeling and wondering if we couldn't focus more on the fact that this is a *community* problem and perhaps an even greater objective than working with individual children.

Summary. Starting from relatively simple observations (lack of reciprocity in making available of information; blocks to communication; lack of clarity in policy and procedure of agencies), this amazing discussion develops into an increasingly focused system-oriented investigation of practical problems in corrections. The systems concept, which nowhere constitutes the manifest focus of this discussion, emerges with increasing clarity with the following components:

(1) *Ad hoc* and systematic case coordination;

(2) Program coordination (and the lack of it);

(3) Physical and human limitations (of agencies);

(4) Position of the individual:
    (a) Institutional constraint
    (b) Operand vs. professed norms
    (c) Effect of the system on the individual;

(5) Adaptation of the worker to the system through understanding of:
    (a) The mission of the system
    (b) The system capabilities and those of its components ("subsystems").

It should be noted that this discussion made no reference to literature or any social work or sociological theories, and certainly not to systems theory. The conception of the correctional field, at which the participants arrived, was developed out of their own experiences and thoughts about their everyday work. To appreciate the performance of this group, its heterogeneity with respect to background should be taken into consideration. In order to follow the fate of the systems concept in this group we will look at their performance the next day (Thursday). Again, we will follow the discussion in some detail.

William Hennessy, Thursday p.m.

The group starts out with a discussion of the effect that professional organizations could have but do not have on the work of correctional officers. It seems that the police officers' association is more successful than correctional officers' organizations in providing them with meaningful contact that would help them in their work, knowledge or professional growth. Existing associations are criticized for not being active enough, not keeping their members up to date, and workers in the field are criticized for being insufficiently interested even to join such an organization. The lack of interest in professional matters on the side of workers in the field could be interpreted as lack of professionalization in corrections. Indicative of this may be the following selection of contributions to the discussion:

X: Are we correctional people part of the system? We follow the system, but are we part of it?

DL: (Giving an historical answer): In 1938 we had the State Probation and Parole Association. Around 1954 they changed their name to Missouri Correctional Association, so the institutional people, police, etc. could be included. Now perhaps there is another change in the opposite direction. Probation officers and institutional people are in separate organizations.

B: I am a little vague on the state's corrections associations.

DL: I think the association itself is a little vague.

B: [Apparently explaining the reasons for his own noninvolvement in the activities of a professional organization]: . . . Maybe I could have been encouraged by my supervisor, but I was not.

Not only the fact of a great many probation officers or related personnel not participating in the life of professional organizations is of interest here, but the lack of motivation to participate and the reasons for it. As reported elsewhere, we did not find any evidence of clarity in the probation officers who were participants in our institute and workshops with respect to their professional roles; the objectives of probation; the question of what criteria to use in the decision of whether or not a case needed to be closed, etc. Also, insufficient salary levels and vagueness of the law with respect to the qualifications of people to be hired as probation officers may contribute to the fact that the field of probation does not attract high-powered professionals or people with adequate role conceptions or loyalty to what they are doing and to one another. The same cannot be said about policemen, and certainly it is not said by the one policeman in the group.

C: The corrections association has progressed exactly down to what we are discussing here: no public relations; no progress; no implementation of the thing that was started; they will not vary their techniques. Corrections people are not part of the group, but a group of their own. They do not present themselves to the community.

We might suspect that they do not present themselves adequately to themselves either, meaning that they cannot function in a professional capacity when their field of endeavor is ill-defined and diffuse.

The discussion then pays some attention to the question of whether the effectiveness of professional organizations might improve in the future. Our policeman addresses himself to that question and adds a comment indicating his belief that informal contacts between correctional workers might be of value:

> C: If they get out here and form committees in these different places and if they will give it some push (they will be successful). If you can get them to eat lunch with each other—we accomplished *more at* [*the campus dormitory*].

The discussion leader then asks people to give the group their impressions of the way or the degree to which they share knowledge or experiences from participation in institutes such as the present one with their colleagues on the job. Various people give various answers, but generally it seems that the efforts of the Institute and the workshops do get spread around. Some people report having formal meetings with their colleagues, others say that they have speaking engagements with groups in the community; one person reports monthly meetings with his local health department where physicians of the department are present, some nurses, the presiding judge of the county court, and FBI agents, representatives from the probate court, from the welfare department, and the juvenile court. The discussion leader then refers to a serious limitation to the imaginative use of resources by probation officers, namely a non-cooperative judge.

> DL: Someone said yesterday or the day before,[8] the one resource you want to get behind is your judge. And we don't have that in [our] City.—Essentially they are against the rotation system of judges. They feel one judge is never there long enough to know juvenile problems.

> C: One half year is not long enough. One year and then rotating is all right. But in my thinking eight years is *too long* to be there. He ceases being judge and becomes a social worker and from then on *you got problems.*

> F: (Illustrates this, apparently, by recounting the case of a boy who, after thirteen confessions including three auto thefts and seven thefts of property over fifty dollars, had never been before a judge): The thing I'm afraid of in some of these juvenile courts is getting exactly what we are getting into in this institute . . .; too much of an NASW slant. Take your panel today; you are getting the do-gooder slant on it. They all think alike. You are getting that do-gooder slant.

The discussion leader recounts his own experiences as a young pro-

---

[8] Meaning in a different Institute Workshop, where he was discussion leader at the time.

fessional worker and the fact that he wondered if he, too, might have been too permissive. This seems to egg on F, who continues ranting:

F: "Give him another chance. He's only snatched a purse from an old lady who had to go without supper. She's probably gone without supper before."

DL: I have a hard time visualizing this coming from a professional person.

We observed before that the professional roles of people active in corrections are insufficiently defined, as are their objectives. Here, something else seems to show itself: the lack of sureness with respect to professional objectives and roles seems to result in anxiety which expresses itself in interdisciplinary hostility. F is not easily pacified and continues to push the discussion in that direction:

F: Think of the panel this morning: There were a lot of words, but nobody said anything—to me. How do you feel about it?

C: They have yet to get down to specifics and say: This you can do. . . People complain about lack of money, and of staff. We have a bunch of excuse makers. For some reason, those people think they can't do anything, yet they take their pay every month. . . But will they go out and do anything? "Give me two weeks to help a child!"—Did you hear that woman ask for two weeks to help a child, that needs help in the next twenty minutes? Why?

Faculty Member of the School of Social Service (who was sitting in as a guest in this discussion): What she meant was, she needs two weeks to find a foster family. They don't find those overnight. They really don't.

C: Doctor, let me ask you this: What are we going to do with this child in those two weeks, eat it? (Then he expounds the view that if the Department of Welfare were looking for foster homes before they needed them, children would not have to go to detention.)

Summarizing the discussion in this session, we observe that the systems concept is still implied in the contributions by various people, although it is not as clearly acknowledged as in the last discussion. Dissatisfaction with the attitude and/or performance of welfare workers is expressed, however, in such a way that we easily see the need for systematization of the correctional process by finding ways to improve the coordination of efforts by various agencies in the field.

Joseph Gorman, Friday a.m.

D: Community relationships can't be accomplished by the individual probation officer. I believe that's where the supervisor, the higher level court agent (comes in). At the individual officer's level, you have to go on the concept of neighborhood effort rather than a city-wide effort.

This quotation by D starts off a discussion characterized by close attention to the practical possibilities available to the worker in the field for the mobilization of community resources. It also shows increasing sophistication in the treatment of available resources. Different job levels, it is suggested, constrain the worker to pay attention to different kinds of neighborhood resources or to different kinds of use that he could make of them. Directly related to this is the following contribution by C:

C: [Reacting to a question about resources and the role of the Missouri Corrections Association]: Social action groups are takers, not givers. They are looking for something for their group, not for you.—(But) there are Optimist Clubs, Kiwanis Clubs, PTA's, all these seem like minor organizations, but they have money and places they can help you with.

A minister itself is good if you are looking for a counselor. If you are looking for funds, a church is not as good, but a council of churches is *excellent*. They again have funds. All you have to do is convince them that you have a good place for money.

You use the civic leaders to spread your needs around the community. [Emphasis added.]

DL: Has anybody else contacted Optimist Clubs?

[Four people say they have, the same four that also contacted Kiwanis Clubs.]

D: [Writing on the blackboard]: I am putting down my experiences, so include me in the handraising [writes names of organizations on the board].

One participant now points out to the group that not only the mere existence of resources is important to note, but that their capabilities may be limited by the relationships that exist between different parts of the social system within which we operate.

B: Let's look at this more realistic. I am a Negro. How do you make contact with an Optimist Club?

C: You mean there are no Negro Optimist Clubs?

B: I know of none.

C: We have a colored officer in our bureau. He is assigned to the same talks as everybody else. If the Optimist Club calls for somebody and it isn't by name, he will be assigned to talk. I make the assignments.

The discussion now takes an interesting turn in that it suggests getting the job done while operating without the system: Since caseloads are as high as they are and people have therefore very little time to make contacts with community resources such as clubs, etc., it appears difficult to mobilize them in behalf of a correctional effort. Several members of the group therefore suggest that the worker make those contacts on his own time. Similar demands also seem to be made occasionally on the representatives of such other agencies as are seen as potentially useful to the corrections effort. C for instance reports that police cars in his city have riders as guests on Fridays and Saturdays: Priests, ministers, and attorneys. This, he says, has been "very useful to us."

DL: In what way?

C: Five priests are counseling for us. Negro attorneys are a resource when we think a child needs a lawyer.

DL: (Asks D to read off the names of organizations that he had put on the blackboard.)

D: There is the Ministerial Alliance or Council of Churches, County and City Child Welfare Advisory Boards, rural area development agencies. There are also alumni associations and groups; (if you dig hard enough, you will find them) and PTA's.

Optimists, Lions, Rotary, Kiwanis . . . these are the individuals who would like to believe that they are contributing to the progress of the community. Each has a vulnerable spot that they desire to be exploited, if you can make a strong enough appeal. We know about Optimists, the friend of the boy. The Lions are involved in sight and hearing. They love to be of assistance in sight and hearing problems. Rotary people help with summer youth activities: Little League, life saving, etc. Kiwanis (I don't remember their weak spot). Business and Professional Women: That's for girls. The Chamber of Commerce consists of young fathers and husbands on the way up who constitute the core of the community . . . in a big city you deal on a neighborhood level, in a small town, on the community level.

After C's observation that any means short of illegal means is worthwhile fighting delinquency, F relapses into some comments concerning judges who would not hire social welfare workers as probation officers because of their attitude toward the judge. The question of salary limitations is also discussed and the difficulty of obtaining instruction in correctional work which will give the student an adequate knowledge of the law.

Summary: Even though the systems concept is hardly mentioned literally, its effect can be traced throughout the Thursday and Friday discussions given above. The observation that workers in corrections have no effective public relations; that there is a lack of interest in the professional activities of that group; that the thinking and the practice of social work may conflict with the needs of the correctional field; that, in fact, the accommodation of needs in the field of corrections by the capabilities of the existing welfare system is "under-organized" to such a degree that hostility exists between various disciplines engaged in this kind of work—all these observations point to the fact that, at least in the minds of the participants in these discussions, there exists already the notion of a *desirable* system, in which needs and capabilities of subsystems will be aligned rationally, organically and effectively. C's suggestion that the State Division of Welfare have a program under which they would have foster homes available at all times, so that they would not have to go looking whenever a particular child needs placement, indicates the direction of that thinking: Decisions can be made in advance, provided it is known in advance what kind of decisions will eventually have to be made. In this example, it is known that sooner or later children will be in need of foster placement. Therefore, by putting foster parents "on call," the time lapse between the occurrence of a need and the action by a subsystem that will meet that need would be minimized. It is a discussion of contingency planning.

The most sophisticated example of "systemic" thought comes from C and D. These two suggest two things:

(1) Community resources have to be judged by their capabilities. They have to be used according to those capabilities. That is, individual problems can be met by individuals (e.g., counselling may be done by ministers willing to cooperate); more generalized needs have to be taken care of by more generalized, i.e., institutionalized, parts of the societal supersystem (e.g., funds can be mobilized by appeal to organizations).

(2) The principle of rational alignment between needs and capabilities of resources extends to the use the correctional worker makes of himself. Thus, the rank and file deputy juvenile officer, with his large caseload and the preponderance of casework demands, should not attempt to organize community resources beyond the neighborhood level, except in very small communities. It is the supervisor or the higher-echelon officer who should take on the task of mobilizing more complex resources such as city-wide, or even the representatives of state-wide, regional, or national organizations. The probation officer "on the beat" is thought to be equipped to handle the two simpler types of inter-agency cooperation in the service of his charges: *Ad hoc* case coordination and systematic case coordination (service integration). Supervisors and administrators are assigned the task of program coordination, i.e., the adjusting of the more complex capabilities of involved, programmed subsystems to the needs, not of individuals, but of groups of individuals, or classes of individuals within the societal supersystem.

FOLLOW-UP WORKSHOP

Resource Person: Forrest Swall

Discussion Leader: Perrian Winget[9]

This follow-up workshop is of interest to us, because its theme directly relates to the motto of our 1964 Summer Institute. The resource person, Mr. Swall, is a former community development agent of the University of Missouri. As in previous summaries of workshops, we will make use of actual contributions to the discussion, quoting as verbatim as is feasible in this transcription of the original tape recording.

The resource person, reviewing for the group a previous workshop, remarks that community organization consists of a theory and the things one actually does. He points out that community organization aims at a balance between needs in a community and available resources; that there are channels of expression that must systematically be used in community organization; that the process involves fact-finding, the planning, initiating, and modifying of a program. Services are established as well as standards of effectiveness of these. The present discussion is to address itself to the actual utilization of community organization principles and techniques in the field of juvenile probation. Mr. Swall quotes from an unpublished paper by Bernard Nash, of the Community Development Division of the University of Missouri. Nash, Mr. Swall reports, finds only six or seven papers in the literature which deal with the *principles of the utilization of resources.*

Following is a listing of some of these principles and some of the group discussion that ensued.

(1) *The resources called upon for utilization should participate in the development of the plan, whatever this plan is going to be.*

This court . . . is notoriously authoritative and final in its . . . decisions.

This is illustrated: Boys Town, when refusing to accept a boy without being filled to capacity, is trying to tell us something: This is a boy who does not fit in their program. However, the rejection of a child referred to a resource may be taken personally. Referring personnel may feel that *they* are rejected, not the child.

An example for proper cooperation and participation of a resource in the treatment plan would be for court personnel to work with the family of a child who has been committed to an institution. Both agencies, in this instance, would constantly be in touch, and the sharing of planning and treatment would establish an atmosphere of cooperation.

The discussion also addresses itself to the fact that at times agencies

[9] Then Juvenile Officer, Mexico, Missouri. Mr. Winget has recently been appointed Executive Director of the Missouri Association for Social Welfare.

are approached reluctantly, in an attempt to let them do the court's job, rather than honestly to engage their services. It is mentioned that "everything is so agency oriented, the child is sometimes forgotten." One contribution to the discussion refers to the process of institutionalization in a social-psychological sense: "In order to solve our problems, we become self-centered."

The discussion, up to this point, has established that the inclusion of resources in the planning process leads to a better on-going relationship. Primary responsibility for including the resource is said to rest with the juvenile court because this is the agency asking for help.

(2) *Community resources should be treated as co-partners rather than subordinates.* They should prepare a description of their specific interests and capacities, participating in the assignment of responsibility for overall program direction. If they do not participate in planning, thorough briefing concerning the purpose of action should precede any requests for help.

The discussion following the presentation of this second principle tends to concentrate on the material limitations of the side of outside agencies. One person mentions that ". . . you have something that is great but you just don't have the time and personnel to follow it through." This is illustrated by the possibility of a child being released from a training school after six months, just because he had behaved well, but not because he is judged as having no further treatment needs. This is seconded by another argument, simply accepting the limitations that exist, to the effect that if a school is overcrowded, "something's gotta give"; but then the discussion recognizes that this still does not meet the child's needs.

At this point the resource person leads the discussion back to its original track, making the point that the very realistic limitations faced by all people in the field are one reason to have common planning initially.

Other limitations are now discussed: Attitudes, jealousy on the side of individuals and institutions, status mindedness, etc., are seen as hurdles to successful cooperation.

C: You on your own hook can get a hell of a lot more done than by asking the judge. . . .

Y: My judge won't be bothered. "Use your own judgment . . ." is what he says. . . .

An increasingly excited discussion ensues, concerning the unavoidable effect which disagreement between the professionals in the field must have on the child.

(3) *The effective use of existing resources is dependent on a clear definition of the need for assistance and (a well defined) expectation of help from each resource.*

This is said to imply a survey of resources. We need to know what is there.

We complain bitterly about resources we do not have but [we] may be unaware of what is there. We need not only the name of institutions on file, but information about them, both in our files and in our heads, so that we really know what kinds of resources they can provide or are providing. *First-hand knowledge is necessary.* We must keep up to date. There must be an on-going pattern of observation.

James Garrett (Project Coordinator in the St. Louis University Institute for Delinquency Control) at this point remarks that corrections is a team effort, and while we have a problem with relationships, much of it is a lack of communication; and that we are pretty threatened by things we do not understand.

Mr. Swall: We have got to know what these resources are and what they have to offer. And we also have to have a pretty good understanding of *what we want from these agencies.*

Reverting back to the systems language which we cautiously introduced before, we might say that the resource person here speaks about the necessity of an alignment of component capabilities and mission requirements.

Mr. Swall then asks whether participants in this workshop have a chance to see the institutions to which they send children. The discussion brings out that most of them do not ever see these institutions. In the case of children who are committed to the State Training School, this act is described as the child being turned over and the officer walking out. One participant suggests that the officer *has* to meet the "social staff."

Mr. Swall re-emphasizes his point that ". . . we can't really make full use of these resources without first-hand knowledge." He suggests that a directory of agencies and institutions be kept by the court, listing all available human and material resources. Consultation of such a directory should be a regular staff function. Apparently, even on the state level, there is no listing available that would be complete with resources of institutions. Available listings give reference to existing programs but are not detailed enough for the needs of the juvenile court. It is suggested that keeping such a directory up to date could be part of a handbook and of an on-going in-service education.

However, not only information about existing resources is needed, but a willingness to accommodate possible differences or, as much as feasible, to align and coordinate the efforts of some of these:

(4) Participating resources should be willing to accept general goals of the juvenile court. Conversely, the juvenile court should grant such resources sufficient flexibility for exercising their judgment. *No singular*

agency should assume unilateral responsibility for a problem or a method of attacking the problem. There should be continuous interaction.

The discussion that follows indicates a gradual acceptance of the "systems-orientation"; institutions rather than individuals are seen as the actors in the community organization drama. Thus, an initial remark by the resource person to the effect that perhaps there exists a lack of empathy with resources, i.e., institutions, is followed up by the discussion leader who observes that "we tend to see the problem from our perspective only. (Also to be recognized are) *over-burdened agencies. . .*" One person suggests that "the court has to take more aggressive leadership . . . " in getting resources to cooperate; and finally, another participant observes that it is ". . . impossible to orient or educate a judge in six months . . .", referring to the *deficiencies inherent in the system* of rotation of judges in the Juvenile Court.

(5) *Any plan for resource utilization should include an estimate of the demands and benefits anticipated, and of the assistance the court can make available to the resource and the barriers and problems likely to be encountered.*

Explaining this, Mr. Swall suggests that at times we might not be aware of the "true" reason behind a recommendation to the judge. We might be trying to get rid of a case from our caseload rather than because of the expected benefits to the child from the treatment or commitment suggested.

Referring to the point concerning barriers and problems likely to be encountered, the discussion centers on the fact that transferring a child to a resource and not giving that distant agency full information on him may circumvent a barrier (e.g., by not letting an agency know that they are not equipped to handle a case) but may also *create* one, when that agency finds out about it. We may consciously or unconsciously play down the problems of a child, in order to get him placed. In the long run, however, Mr. Swall points out, we have got to be honest. Reason:

(6) *The agency serving a child must have confidence in all other agencies whose cooperation is requested.*

In other words, there must be respect between agencies, and that respect must be demonstrated, e.g., by accepting an agency's refusal to treat when a child does not fit in their program and conversely, an institution has to respect a judge's decision even though it may seem inappropriate to that agency.

3. Discussion: The Systems Concept as Viewed by Practitioners in Probation.

Just as in at least two of the workshops in the Summer Institute, in this Follow-up Workshop we find reference to a "real" and also to an "ideal" system operating in the area of juvenile corrections. On the "reality" level, we have the problem of how to find enough time, caseloads being what they are, to learn about resources and cultivate relationships with them. The pressures of the job partly defeat its purpose by institutionalizing the probation officer, in the sense that he becomes self-centered, preoccupied with the immediate, and unaware of the "mission," i.e., the tasks, of the correctional system as a whole.

These limitations are recognized by workshop participants. Some suggest that a probation officer *has* to establish contact with the appropriate staff of treatment facilities, training schools, etc.; others observe that under present circumstances, work on an eight-hour day basis will not do justice to the needs of children.

Implied in this is the image of an "ideal" state of affairs, as a standard, a correctional system with the following characteristics:

Human and material resources of all participants in the correctional process are matched to the needs of the client, either by making appropriate referrals, or by developing new resources.

This means that every agency or facility invited to cooperate with the court must be used within its known resources with respect to the demands which we may want to make on them. In the dealings between the court and other agencies, certain objective and attitudinal factors need to be taken into consideration:

(1) *Objective factors.* Court personnel have to be clear about their needs and must obtain from other helping facilities relevant information about their resources. Needs on the side of the court (representing, as it were, the social attempt at rehabilitation) are of two kinds:

a) general needs, stemming from the overall aims of the correctional system;

b) specific needs, diagnosed by the probation officer with respect to an individual client. *These must be articulated and openly discussed with the accepting agency.*

Knowledge about an agency's resources and limitations comes from contact with the agency, e.g., through an understanding of the reasons for refusal in specific cases.

(2) *Attitudinal factors.* There should be mutual acceptance between the juvenile court and outside community resources. There must be *empathy* for agencies (e.g., understanding of institutional constraint, i.e., the way in which individuals functioning within an institution are limited in their choices for action by the aims and purposes of that institution).

4. Comparison of Contents Between the 1963 and 1964 Institute Workshops.

The main difference between the Institutes of 1963 and 1964 was that the former offered different perspectives of the traditional functions of diagnosis and treatment and the latter was organized around a central theme which constitutes an orientation not yet very much developed in practice. Since probation is dominated by the casework method, it cannot be expected to have paid too much attention to the need for, the possibility, or the techniques of community involvement.

We were interested to see whether this difference would be reflected in the way Institute materials were handled in the workshops. It was.

Tables 1 and 2 contain the raw data for this comparison (unless one were to consider the recordings themselves as such). Tables 3 and 4 make the comparison easier, as the proportional incidence of all themes is given, workshop by workshop, in addition to the absolute number of responses or exchanges relating to them.

Tables 5 and 6 add another dimension to the comparison. It can be noticed that the Proportional Incidence values of most themes changed but little during the week of the 1963 Institute. The exceptions (*systems thought* and *social sanction*) which do show a fairly consistent increase and decline, respectively, are in the direction in which one would like to see it go from the point of view of training for systematic work. Most of the figures seem to indicate that, while there were fluctuations in the relative attention to different areas of knowledge and practice, the tone of the 1963 Institute was not changed very much as it progressed.

In 1964, by contrast, there seems to be evidence of a "career" of areas of attention. Concern with professionalism and systems thought shows marked increases, mostly at the expense of attention paid to social structure and function. The explanation of this might well be a shift, during the Institute, from understanding to action, or from diagnosis to systematic treatment, from theory to application. If so, this development is especially noteworthy considering that in 1964, there was no planned division of program days into diagnostic and therapeutic topical elements. Thus we may interpret these results as evidence that the participants did what we had hoped they would: absorb some of the materials presented first, then work them over and explore the new knowledge in the light of the demands and possibilities of their own work.

Table 7 introduces still another element into our analysis. The thematic categories were ordered by their ΣN (sum of their workshop-by-workshop frequencies) in 1964. The following should be noted: No's 1, 2, and 3, *professionalism, systems thought* and *social structure and function* are all large, higher level abstraction themes, comprising a greater number of specifics than No's 4, 5, and 6, *economics, social sanction,* and *psychodynamics* (at least when seen from the point of view of corrections). This being so, there is a natural bias in our scoring: More responses can be expected to contribute to themes 1, 2, and 3 than to the others. The result of $\Sigma N=138$ for the 1963 integrating themes as against

68 for the differentiating themes might in itself be meaningless. Comparison with the 1964 results (156 vs. 9), however, illustrates again how much more focused on complexities, "integrations" (as contrasted with specifics, eg., differential causes of delinquency) the 1964 discussions were.

Graph 1 merely repeats the data listed in Table 7 in visual form.

For easier comparison, here is an excerpt from Table 7:

	1963	1964
Integrating Themes (Sum of 1, 2, 3)	138	156
Differentiating Themes (Sum of 4, 5, 6)	68	9

Figure 3: Total Incidence (ΣN) of Integrating and Differentiating Themes by Year of Institute.

CONTENT ANALYSIS OF WORKSHOPS

SUMMER INSTITUTE 1963

Table 1a

Monday—One Workshop (Hardman)

Themes Discussed:

1. *Professionalism, competence in probation (0)*[10]

2. *Systems thought (1)*
   child as gestalt

3. *Social structure and function (5)*
   communication between social agencies
   economy of good communication
   stigma of institutionalization
   role
   conflict of roles (police *vs.* social work)

4. *Economics (0)*

[10] Numbers in parentheses indicate frequency of occurrence in any one workshop.

5. *Social sanction (3)*
law
authority
punishment

6. *Psychodynamics (0)*

Table 1b

Tuesday A.M. Reefer

1. *Professionalism, competence in probation (1)*
limits of the probation officer's competence

2. *Systems thought (6)*
multiplicity of causes
social complexity
self-image as function of society
demands *vs.* opportunity
economics (economy eliminating jobs)
differential unemployment

3. *Social structure and function (8)*
anomie
social complexity
self-image as function of society
class bias in probation
demands *vs.* opportunity
parents and social pressures
decreasing family unity
differential unemployment

4. *Economics (3)*
economics (economy eliminating jobs)
employment (as unmanageable social force)
differential unemployment

5. *Social sanction (1)*
class bias in probation

6. *Psychodynamics (7)*
motivation
wish to get caught
wish to get punished
impulse
unplanned (irrational) violence
"blinders"
enuresis

Table 1c

Tuesday P.M. Reefer

1. *Professionalism, competence in probation (9)*
   belief systems underlying treatment, e.g., free will *vs.* determinism
   self-awareness and bias
   use of available time
   limitations, of space and time, reducing thoroughness of diagnosis
   variation of practice (judge's influence)
   caseload *vs.* workload
   probation objectives
   division of labor in probation
   confidentiality

2. *Systems thought (4)*
   the child in social context
   limitations in space and time as reducing thoroughness of diagnosis
   diagnosis—unilateral?
   division of labor in probation

3. *Social structure and function (3)*
   home
   limitations: lack of services locally
                lack of specialized services

4. *Economics (9)*
   needs of probationers
   limitations on facilities (availability)
   inappropriate use of facilities
   limitations: lack of services locally
                lack of specialized services
                money
   promise of technology (e.g., information storage facilities for record
     keeping)
   variation in workload
   caseload *vs.* workload

5. *Social sanction (7)*
   centralization of treatment
   appropriate use of training schools
   training schools as last resort
   standardization of court practice
   timing of commitment (chances of rehabilitation)
   limitations (no time) of service
   variation in workload

6. *Psychodynamics (1)*
   timing of commitment (chances for rehabilitation)

Table 1d

Tuesday P.M. Winget

1. *Professionalism, competence in probation (15)*
   objectives of probation
   probation officer as goal setter
   contents of treatment
   who sets standards for action?
   artificiality of interview situation
   objectivity
   probation officer's affect
   probation officer's ego involvement and frustration
   working relationships as more important than goals
   feedback
   consistency in rule enforcement
   purpose of social investigation
   knowledge as goal-directed
   functional approach
   attention to assets, resources, strengths rather than "causes"

2. *Systems thought (1)*
   feedback: treatment influenced by behavioral change in client. Influence of probation officer's attitude and feelings.

3. *Social structure and function (7)*
   institutional constraint (function set by agency)
   institutional constraint (strictness of officer depending on judge)
   responsibility (judge as decision-maker)
   inadequacy of formal commitment to rules
   flexibility of rules: client centered
   difficulty of internalization of rules in an authoritative setting (lack of choice)
   roles of probation officer and client

4. *Economics (0)*

5. *Social sanction (2)*
   function of court
   enabling *vs.* restrictive treatment

6. *Psychodynamics (8)*
   treatment planning

prediction of post-supervision behavior
probation officer's affect
probation officer's ego involvement and frustration
influence of client's movement on probation officer's attitude
flexibility of rules: client centered
value formation as internalization of rules
difficulty of internalizing rules in authoritative setting

Table 1e

Wednesday A.M. Winget

1. *Professionalism, competence in probation (10)*
   application of theory
   utility of theory
   utility of theory: makes practice effective
   qualification of probation officer as limiting factor
   selection of information as subject to school of thought
   probation officer's responsibility as related to capacity
   impact and responsibility of probation officer
   community participation in probation
   selectiveness in seeking cooperation
   education of the public

2. *Systems thought (1)*
   variations in the complexity of problems and their treatment

3. *Social structure and function (8)*
   the client as gestalt, in space and time
   institutional constraint: application of theoretical knowledge
   variations in the complexity of problems and their treatment
   community power structure
   variations in cooperation
   selectiveness in seeking cooperation
   education of the public
   community participation in probation

4. *Economics (0)*

5. *Social sanction (2)*
   probation officer's responsibility as related to capacity
   impact and responsibility of probation officer

6. *Psychodynamics (2)*
   the client as gestalt, in space and time
   variations in the complexity of problems and their treatment

Table 1f

Wednesday P.M. O'Brien

1. *Professionalism, competence in probation (13)*
   probation officer's needs and affect
   variations in style and bias among probation officers
   stereotype in diagnosis
   "objectivity": does it leave out the child's affect?
   relevance of information: (a) as controlled by availability of resources
       for treatment, (b) controlled by the needs of the child, (c) controlled
       by anticipated needs later or for others
   formal *vs.* empathetic perspective
   difficulty of decision-getting
   interdisciplinary approach
   need for integration of diverse ideas
   meaning of integration
   question of competence
   social as undefined
   humility *vs.* self-assurance

2. *Systems thought (3)*
   interpersonal nature of "meaning"
   feedback as necessary for understanding
   distortion of meaning and perception within and between people

3. *Social structure and function (6)*
   culture and personality
   social determination of one's "stand"
   interpersonal nature of "meaning"
   feedback as necessary for understanding
   distortion of meaning and perception within and between people
   limitations: institutional constraint

4. *Economics (0)*

5. *Social sanction (1)*
   limitations: institutional constraints (probation officer's recommenda-
       tions may be ignored by judge or community)

6. *Psychodynamics (9)*
   probation officer's needs and affect
   affected empathy
   "objectivity"; does it leave out the child's affect?
   culture and personality
   interpersonal nature of meaning
   feedback as necessary for understanding

distortion of meaning and perception within and between people
the child as gestalt
humility *vs.* self-assurance

Table 1g

Thursday A.M. Hardman

1. *Professionalism, competence in probation (4)*
   means *vs.* ends
   ad hoc resources and solutions
   structure of control
   gestalt view as prerequisite for diagnosis

2. *Systems thought (1)*
   understanding from the youngster's point of view

3. *Social structure and function (7)*
   cultural determinacy
   juvenile delinquency as potentially superior adjustment
   gestalt view as prerequisite for diagnosis
   ad hoc resources and solutions
   context: significance of community attitude
   context: social class, value discrepancies
   social change as desideratum

4. *Economics (0)*

5. *Social sanction (1)*
   structure of control

6. *Psychodynamics (3)*
   understanding from the youngster's point of view
   juvenile delinquency as potentially superior adjustment
   motivational change

Table 1h

Thursday A.M. Winget

1. *Professionalism, competence in probation (2)*
   social context and diagnosis
   children as a resource

2. *Systems thought (2)*
   social context and diagnosis
   children as resources

3. *Social structure and function (1)*
   social context and diagnosis

4. *Economics (0)*

5. *Social sanction (0)*

6. *Psychodynamics (1)*
   lack of initiative

Table 1i

Thursday P.M. Winget

1. *Professionalism, competence in probation (11)*
   overwork of probation officers
   necessity of work with families
   allotment of resources (who needs us most?)
   criteria for choosing objectives
   rejection of criteria: each case is unique
   probation officer's role
   probation officer as confidant
   probation officer as mediator between child and society
   probation officer as developer of the child's potential
   probation officer as buffer between the child and the police
   probation officer as advisor to the court

2. *Systems thought (5)*
   necessity of work with families
   underlying problems
   situation and indicated treatment
   allotment of resources (who needs us most?)
   probation officer as mediator between child and society

3. *Social structure and function (5)*
   function of the court
   court as scarecrow
   limitations of court function
   allotment of resources (who needs us most?)
   probation officer as mediator between child and society

4. *Economics (1)*
   allotment of resources (who needs us most?)

5. *Social sanction (3)*
   function of the court
   limitations of court function
   court as scarecrow

6. *Psychodynamics (4)*
   intuition
   boost of client's initiative
   probation officer's role as confidant
   probation officer as developer of the child's potential

CONTENT ANALYSIS OF WORKSHOPS
SUMMER INSTITUTE 1964

Table 2a

Monday A.M. Mullins

Themes discussed:

1. *Professionalism, competence in probation (2)*
   sociological terminology
   worker as a model

2. *Systems thought (0)*

3. *Social structure and function (3)*
   role in family
   juvenile delinquent: change over time
   role of juvenile court

4. *Economics (0)*

5. *Social sanction (1)*
   role of juvenile court

6. *Psychodynamics (0)*

Table 2b

Monday P. M. Mullins

1. *Professionalism, competence in probation (11)*
   procedure in probation
   court procedure and purpose
   juvenile code: variation of procedure
                   implementation
   law *vs.* social work
   probation officer and community
   agreement among probation officers on purpose of probation
   control *vs.* treatment

probation *vs.* residential treatment
responsibility to society
adverse publicity
public relations

2. *Systems thought (0)*

3. *Social structure and function (8)*
purpose of juvenile court
court procedure and purpose
juvenile code: variation of procedure
                    implementation
probation officer and community
community pressure
resources
adverse publicity
public relations

4. *Economics (0)*

5. *Social sanction (3)*
purpose of juvenile court
control *vs.* treatment
probation *vs.* residential treatment

6. *Psychodynamics (0)*

Table 2c

Tuesday A.M. Roberts

1. *Professionalism, competence in probation (5)*
cooperation between agencies
sharing of information as harmful to child
use of resources in schools
bureaucracy limiting competence
non-use of available information

2. *Systems thought (2)*
cooperation between agencies
development of facilities

3. *Social structure and function (5)*
bureaucracy limiting competence
function of school
education as a generic concept
school as offering variety of services
ethics of educational experiments

4. *Economics (0)*

5. *Social sanction (0)*

6. *Psychodynamics (0)*

Table 2d

Tuesday P.M. Roberts

1. *Professionalism, competence in probation (9)*
   mobilization of resources
   confidentiality
   knowledge of the school
   limitation: caseload
   communication between correctional and other agencies
   lack of communication
   areas of concern for court
   passing the buck

2. *Systems thought (5)*
   mobilization of resources
   utility of schools as resources
   communication between correctional and other agencies
   passing the buck
   lack of communication

3. *Social structure and function (2)*
   mobilization of resources
   competence of police

4. *Economics (0)*

5. *Social sanction (0)*

6. *Psychodynamics (0)*

Table 2e

Wednesday P.M. Swall

1. *Professionalism, competence in probation (29)*
   confidentiality
   time pressure
   ad hoc case coordination
   mission
   inter-agency non-coordination

institutional constraint
limitations: budget, people, training
empathy with outside agency
professed *vs.* operand norms
police and court as only resources on tap
procedures: utilization of resources
personal *vs.* agency relationship
blocks to communication
procedure change: friction; misunderstood system change
lack of clarity in procedure
lack of even case coordination
obstacles: dissolution by working with them
community organization techniques: organization of resources
creation of resources
popular education *re* community needs and action
community organization techniques: organization of resources, eliciting
   initiative in resources
court and police: leadership in community
procurement of resources
leadership in procurement
specificity in procurement leadership ("who takes the initiative")
vagueness of concept of "resource"
difficulties to enforce the law
concept of "community effort" as hard to grasp

2. *Systems thought (26)*
   reciprocity in cooperation
   mission
   inter-agency non-coordination
   institutional constraint
   information flow
   empathy with outside agency
   police and court as only resources on tap
   procedure: utilization of resources
   personal *vs.* agency relationships
   blocks to communication
   procedure change: friction; misunderstood system change
   right to information on system change
   parataxis
   lack of clarity in procedure
   lack of even case coordination
   fragmentation of resources
   lack of coordination
   remedial action to establish coordination
   community organization techniques: organization of resources

creation of resources
popular education *re* community needs and action
community organization techniques: organization of resources, eliciting
    initiative in resources
procurement of resources
leadership in procurement
learning from children

3. *Social structure and function (4)*
sin *vs.* crime
rural-urban differences
court and police: leadership role in community
cooperation of parents

4. *Economics (1)*
leadership in procurement

5. *Social sanction (0)*

6. *Psychodynamics (1)*
probation officer's affect

Table 2f

Wednesday P.M. Gorman

1. *Professionalism, competence in probation (5)*
how to win cooperation
cooperation: procedure
initiative
procurement of resources
professional competence and price

2. *Systems thought (4)*
how to win cooperation
cooperation: procedure
utility of resources
procurement of resources

3. *Social structure and function (0)*

4. *Economics (1)*
procurement of resources

5. *Social sanction (0)*

6. *Psychodynamics (0)*

Table 2g

Thursday P.M. Hennessy

1. *Professionalism, competence in probation (15)*
   communication in the profession
   getting movement among professionals
   motivation for professional exchanges
   correctional people: part of the system?
   vagueness of correctional association
   lack of participation in professional organization
   efficacy of professional organization
   motivation to participate as function of informal contacts
   exchange of information (learning) with colleagues not attending
   exchange of information as mutual help
   judge *vs.* social worker
   lack of service integration (interprofessional hostility)
   corrections *vs.* social worker
   need for operationalization (gap between conceptual and empirical
      training)
   exchange of information with other professions

2. *Systems thought (5)*
   getting movement among professionals
   correctional people: part of the system?
   efficacy of professional organization
   lack of service integration (interprofessional hostility)
   systematization, programmed service

3. *Social structure and function (7)*
   cohesiveness among police
   motivation to participate as function of informal contacts
   limitations: judge is not alway a resource
   judge *vs.* social worker
   corrections *vs.* social work
   social work as do-gooderism
   lack of service integration (interprofessional hostility)

4. *Economics (0)*

5. *Social sanction (0)*

6. *Psychodynamics (0)*

Table 2h

Friday Gorman

1. *Professionalism, competence in probation (9)*
   functional differentiations of professional levels
   organization as resource
   making contact with organizations
   high caseloads *vs.* systematic work
   ad hoc case coordination
   roster of resources
   motivation of agency
   judge *vs.* social worker
   shortcomings of training for corrections

2. *Systems thought (5)*
   functional differentiation of professional levels
   making contact with organizations
   high caseloads *vs.* systematic work
   roster of resources
   motivation of agency

3. *Social structure and function (3)*
   organized need (social action groups)
   organization as resource
   judge *vs.* social worker

4. *Economics (2)*
   organized need (social action groups)
   organization as resource

5. *Social sanction (0)*

6. *Psychodynamics (0)*

INSTITUTE WORKSHOPS, 1963

Table 3

Themes Discussed

Categories:

1. Professionalism, Competence of Professional Corrections Workers
2. Systems Thought
3. Social Structure and Function
4. Economics
5. Social Sanction
6. Psychodynamics

Workshop	Category No.	N	Proportional Incidence
Monday P.M. Hardman n=9	1	0	0
	2	1	11.5
	3	5	55.5
	4	0	0
	5	3	33
	6	0	0
Tuesday A.M. Reefer n=19	1	1	5.3
	2	6	31.5
	3	8	42
	4	3	15.4
	5	1	5.3
	6	7	36.8
Tuesday P.M. Reefer n=26	1	9	34.6
	2	4	15.4
	3	3	11.6
	4	9	34.6
	5	7	27
	6	1	3.8
Tuesday P.M. Winget n=26	1	15	57.8
	2	1	3.8
	3	7	26.8
	4	0	0
	5	2	7.7
	6	8	30.8

(Table 3 continued on next page)

(Table 3 Continued)

Workshop	Category No.	N	Proportional Incidence
Wednesday A.M. Winget n=15	1	10	66.7
	2	1	6.7
	3	8	53.2
	4	0	0
	5	2	13.4
	6	2	13.4
Wednesday P.M. O'Brien n=21	1	13	62.0
	2	3	14.3
	3	5	23.8
	4	0	0
	5	1	4.7
	6	9	42.8
Thursday A.M. Hardman n=11	1	4	36.4
	2	1	9.1
	3	7	63.7
	4	0	0
	5	1	9.1
	6	3	27.3
Thursday A.M. Winget n=3	1	2	66.7
	2	2	66.7
	3	1	33.3
	4	0	0
	5	0	0
	6	1	33.3
Thursday P.M. Winget n=18	1	11	61.1
	2	5	27.8
	3	5	27.8
	4	1	55.6
	5	3	16.6
	6	4	22.2

INSTITUTE WORKSHOPS, 1964

Table 4

Themes Discussed

Categories:

1. Professionalism, Competence of Professional Corrections Workers
2. Systems Thought
3. Social Structure and Function
4. Economics
5. Social Sanction
6. Psychodynamics

Workshop	Category No.	N	Proportional Incidence
Monday A.M. Mullins—III n=5	1	2	40
	2	0	0
	3	3	60
	4	0	0
	5	1	20
	6	0	0
Monday P.M. Mullins—III n=13	1	10	77.0
	2	0	0
	3	7	53.9
	4	0	0
	5	3	23.1
	6	0	0
Tuesday A.M. Roberts—III n=8	1	3	37.5
	2	2	25.0
	3	5	62.5
	4	0	0
	5	0	0
	6	0	0
Tuesday P.M. Roberts—III n=10	1	8	80.0
	2	5	50.0
	3	2	20.0
	4	0	0
	5	0	0
	6	0	0

(Table 4 continued on next page)

(Table 4 continued)

Workshop	Category No.	N	Proportional Incidence
Wednesday P.M. Gorman n=6	1	5	83.3
	2	4	66.7
	3	0	0
	4	1	16.6
	5	0	0
	6	0	0
Wednesday P.M. Swall—III n=40	1	29	72.5
	2	25	62.6
	3	4	10
	4	1	2.5
	5	0	0
	6	1	2.5
Thursday P.M. Hennessy—III n=17	1	14	82.3
	2	5	29.4
	3	6	35.4
	4	0	0
	5	0	0
	6	0	0
Friday Gorman—III n=10	1	9	90
	2	5	50
	3	3	30
	4	2	20
	5	0	0
	6	0	

Table 5: Proportional Incidence* of Thematic Categories, By Day of Institute, 1963.

Thematic Category	Monday	Tuesday	Wednesday	Thursday	Friday
1. Professionalism, Competence of Professional Corrections Workers	0	35.2	64	34.4	—
2. Systems Thought	11.5	15.5	11.2	25.0	—
3. Social Structure and Function	55.5	25.4	36.2	40.7	—
4. Economics	0	16.9	0	3.1	—
5. Social Sanction	33.0	14.1	8.3	12.5	—
6. Psychodynamics	0	22.6	30.5	25.0	—

Table 6: Proportional Incidence of Thematic Categories, By Day of Institute, 1964

Thematic Category	Monday	Tuesday	Wednesday	Thursday	Friday
1. Professionalism, Competence of Professional Corrections Workers	66.7	63.0	74.0	82.3	90.9
2. Systems Thought	0	36.8	63.0	29.4	50.0
3. Social Structure and Function	55.6	36.8	8.7	35.4	30.0
4. Economics	0	0	4.4	0	20.0
5. Social Sanction	22.2	0	0	0	0
6. Psychodynamics	0	0	2.2	0	0

Proportional Incidence is here, and in Table 6, defined as 100 $\frac{\Sigma N}{\Sigma n}$, where ΣN and Σn are the sums of responses and exchanges recorded during an entire day. For definition of N and n, see page 96, on method.

Table 7

COMPARISON BETWEEN 1963 AND 1964 INSTITUTES

Thematic Category	1963		1964		Proportional Change (1963=100)
	ΣN	Prop. Incid.	ΣN	Prop. Incid.	
1. Professionalism, Competence of Professional Corrections Workers	65	43.9	80	73.4	167
2. Systems Thought	24	16.2	46	42.2	260
3. Social Structure and Function	49	33.2	30	27.6	83
4. Economics	13	8.8	4	3.7	42
5. Social Sanction	20	13.5	4	3.7	27
6. Psychodynamics	35	23.7	1	0.9	4
	Σn=148		Σn=109		
Integrating Themes (Sum of 1, 2, 3)	138	93.3	156	143.2	154
Differentiating Themes (Sum of 4, 5, 6)	68	45.6	9	8.3	18

CONTENT ANALYSIS OF WORKSHOP DISCUSSIONS
COMPARISON BETWEEN 1963 and 1964 SUMMER INSTITUTES

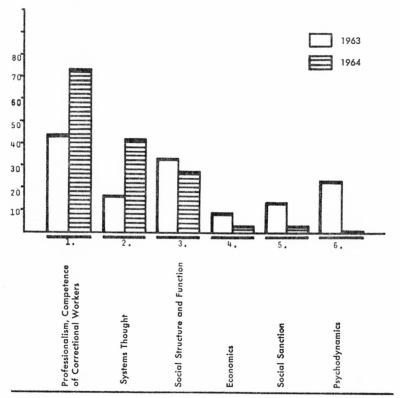

Graph 1: Relative prepotency of discussion themes, by proportional incidence.

5. Conclusion

In our 1964 Institute for Juvenile Correctional and Related Personnel, a group of practitioners were exposed to some of the ideas connected with the notion that *corrections is a community effort*. The Institute lasted five days, during which the participants had ample opportunity to react to the material presented to them. As part of our evaluation, a content analysis of the sessions of one of the discussion groups and of one Follow-Up Workshop session was made, based on tape recordings of the discussions. Four features of these discussions seem to stand out in particular: (1) The participants, coming from a variety of agencies, are able and willing to listen to each other and understand each other's capacities and limitations. (2) Mutual understanding and focusing on the theme of the 1964 Institute increased markedly during the week, suggesting that cross-institutional get-togethers of this kind are useful and needed. (3) The idea of "institutional constraint" (though not called by that name), i.e., the notion that individual capacities and motives are at least partially dominated by the apparatus within which a worker operates, are familiar to them, so that the view of society, or subcultures, and of corrections *as systems* is likely to be comprehensible, not only to academicians, but also to people concerned with practice. (4) The material brought out in these discussions, when taken as a valid reflection of juvenile corrections as presently operating, suggests *an urgent necessity to align component capabilities and needs stemming from general and specific requirements inherent in the "mission" of the correctional supersystem. There are suboptimization about casework and serious deficiencies in the information flow between components of the system, leading to unnecessary and harmful ignorance, misjudgment or mutual distrust among the unintegrated parts, thus inhibiting the organization of work in corrections.*

We offer this analysis as an illustration of what might be done right now to work towards the systematization of the corrections field, by way of in-service training. It is a record of one aspect (with which we were pleased) of our project and hopefully will be a stimulus to others engaged in similar efforts.

Bibliography

Benne, Kenneth D., "Deliberate Changing as the Facilitation of Growth," *The Planning of Change*, New York: Holt, Rinehart, and Winston (1961)

Bowman, Addison M., "Appeals from Juvenile Courts," *Crime and Delinquency*, National Council on Crime and Delinquency, Vol. XI, No. 1 (January 1965)

Chein, Isador, *Studies on Narcotic Use Among Juveniles*, Research Center for Human Relations, New York University (1956)

Cloward, Richard A. and Lloyd E. Ohlin, *New Perspective on Juvenile Delinquency*, New York School of Social Work, Columbia University (1959)

Council on Social Work Education, *Casebook in Correctional Work*, New York: Council on Social Work Education (1959)

Frank, Jerome, *Law and the Modern Mind*, Garden City, New York: Doubleday & Company, Inc. (1963)

Geis, Gilbert and Herbert A. Bloch, *Man, Crime and Society*, New York: Random House (1962)

Gibbons, Donald C., "Some Notes on Treatment Theory in Corrections," *The Social Service Review*, Chicago: The University of Chicago Press, September (1962), Vol. XXXVI, No. 3

Gilman, Merritt and Alice M. Low, *Training for Juvenile Probation Officers*, Children's Bureau Publication No. 398 (1962)

Glueck, Sheldon, "Roscoe Pound and Criminal Justice," *Crime and Delinquency*, National Council on Crime and Delinquency, Vol. X, No. 4 (October 1964)

Holden, Gerald M., St. Louis University School of Social Service, *An Attempt at Training and Demonstration in Juvenile Probation*. Paper presented at the 91st Annual Forum of the National Conference on Social Welfare, Los Angeles (May 1964)

Kahl, Joseph A., *The American Class Structure*, New York, Rinehart (1957)

Kahn, Alfred, *Planning Community Services for Children in Trouble*, New York, Columbia University Press (1963)

Kluckhohn, Clyde and Henry A. Murray, *Personality In Nature, Society and Culture*, New York, Knopf (1948)

Maslow, Abram, *Motivation and Personality*, New York, Harper (1954)

McCune, Shirley D., and Daniel L. Skoler, "Juvenile Court Judges in the United States, Part I: A National Profile," *Crime and Delinquency*, National Council on Crime and Delinquency, Vol. XI, No. 2 (April 1965)

Mead, Margaret, "Social Change and Cultural Surrogates," *Journal of Educational Sociology*, Vol. 14 (1940)

Miles, Arthur P., "The Reality of the Probation Officer's Dilemma," *Federal Probation*, Vol. 29, No. 1 (March 1965)

Missouri, *Juvenile Code* (1957)

Morris, Charles W., Introduction to George H. Mead, *Mind, Self, and Society*, Chicago, University of Chicago Press (1934)

142

National Institute of Mental Health and Children's Bureau, U.S. Dept. of Health, Education and Welfare, *Report to the Congress on Juvenile Delinquency*, Washington, D.C.: U.S. Government Printing Office (1957)

Parsons, Talcott, "A Sociologist Looks at the Legal Profession," in *Essays in Sociological Theory*, Glencoe, Free Press (1954)

Parsons, Talcott, *The Structure of Social Action*, Glencoe, Free Press (1949)

Reid, William, "Interagency Co-ordination in Delinquency Prevention and Control," *Social Service Review*, Vol. XXXVIII, No. 4 (December 1964)

Studt, Elliot, *A Conceptual Approach to Teaching Materials*, New York: Council on Social Work Education (March 1965)

————, "Correctional Services (Social Work Practice In)," *Encyclopedia of Social Work*, Vol. XV, National Association of Social Workers (1965)

Treger, Harvey, "Reluctance of the Social Agency to Work with the Offender," *Federal Probation*, Vol. 28, No. 1 (March 1965)

Tylor, Sir E. B., *Primitive Culture*, quoted here from Melville P. Herskovits, *Cultural Anthropology*, New York, Knopf (1958)

Whyte, William Foote, "A Slum Sex Code," *American Journal of Sociology*, Vol. 49 (July 1943)

Younghusband, Eileen L., "The Dilemma of the Juvenile Court." Reproduced with Permission by the U.S. Dept. of Health, Education, and Welfare, *Social Service Review*, Chicago: The University of Chicago Press (March 1959)